Mandala Adult Coloring Book

Over 50 Calming, Stress Relieving Designs

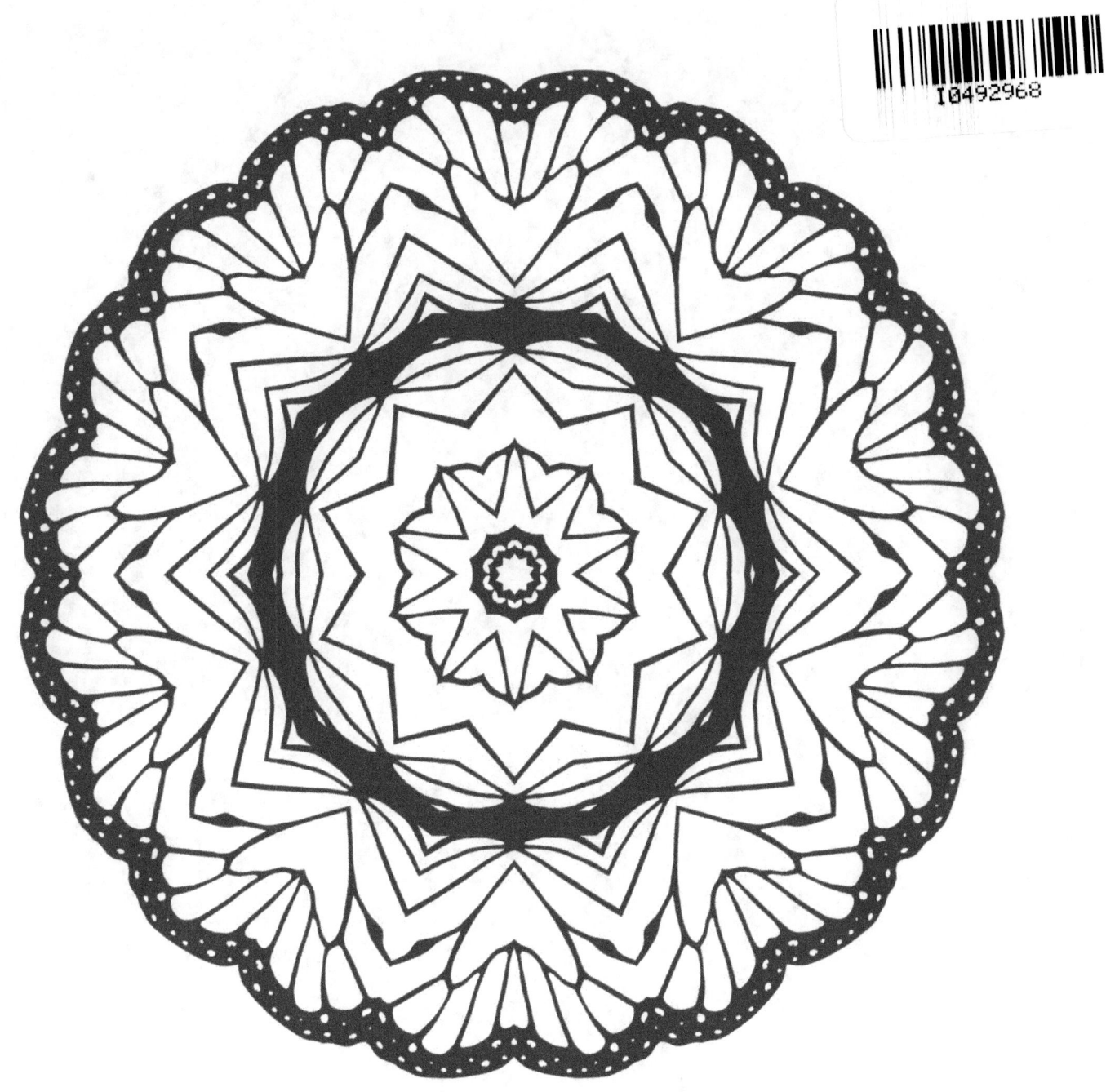

Illustrated by Lisa Higgins

Published in 2016 by
Miss Higgs Published Collection
Perth, Western Australia
www.misshiggspublishedcollection.com

1st Edition 2016

ISBN:
ISBN-13: 978 1533337733
ISBN-10: 153333773X

Printed by Create Space

Designs by Lisa Higgins

DEDICATION

This book is dedicated to
my wonderful and supportive family, in its entirety, love you all.

Welcome...

Welcome to Mandala Adult Coloring Book, this book offers a collection of intricate mandalas for you to personalize.

The Mandala is a religious symbol representing the universe. Traditionally it is used by Buddhists as a meditative tool. However it is featured in a number of religious and psychological practiced for representing balance and contemplation amongst other things.

Directions

A test page has been included at the front of the book for you to test your markers for color or bleed. We would also recommend inserting a blank sheet of paper behind the page you are working on. Each illustration has been printed on a single page to ensure you are not ruining another image behind it with any marker bleeding, alternatively if you choose to frame the work at a later date you don't have to choose between your images.

I hope you enjoy this collection.

WOULD YOU LIKE AN ADULT COLORING IN PRINTABLE?

Please visit www.misshiggspublishedcollection.com and subscribe to our weekly newsletter to receive your free adult coloring in printables.

Test Page

Use this test page before coloring your illustrations.

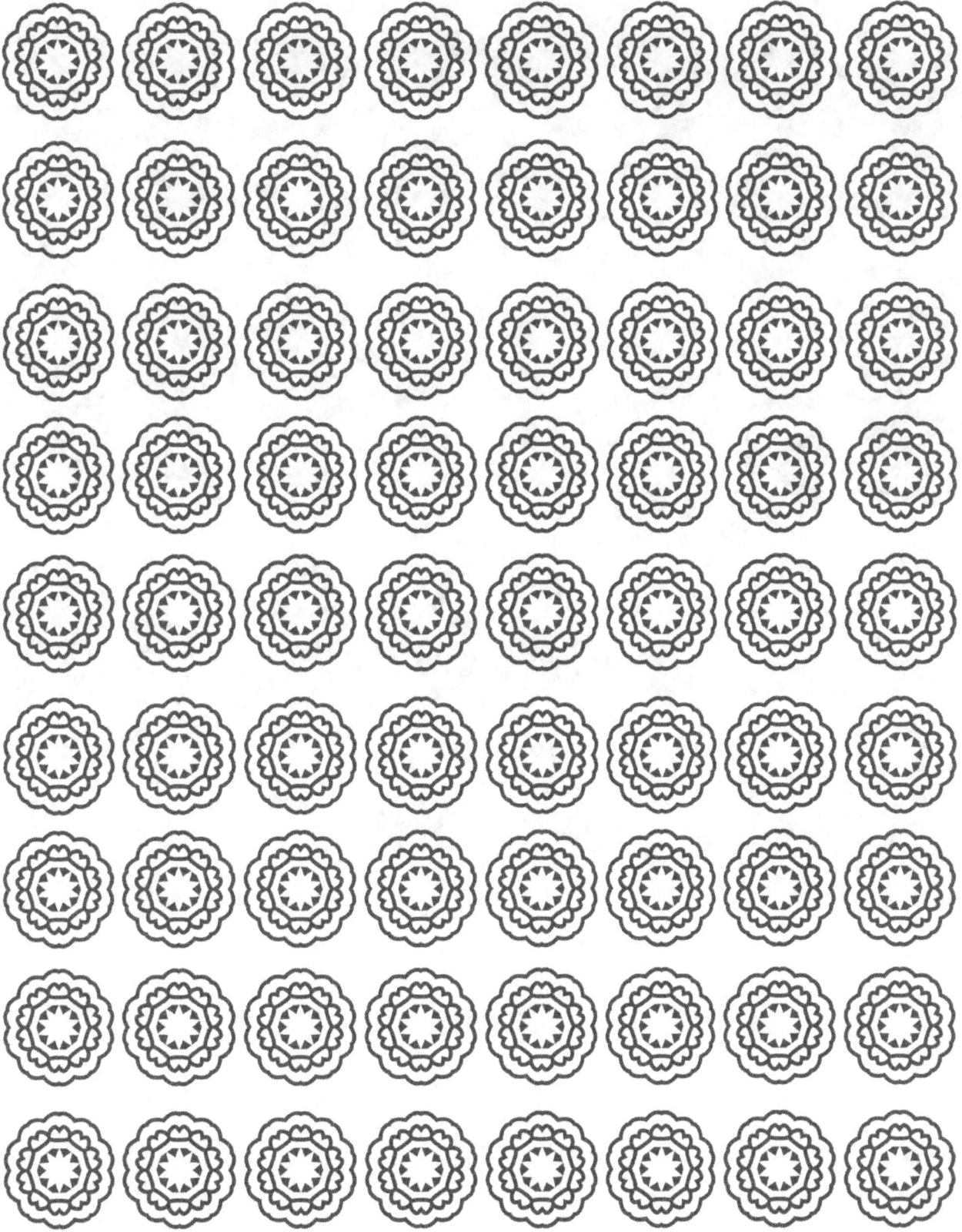

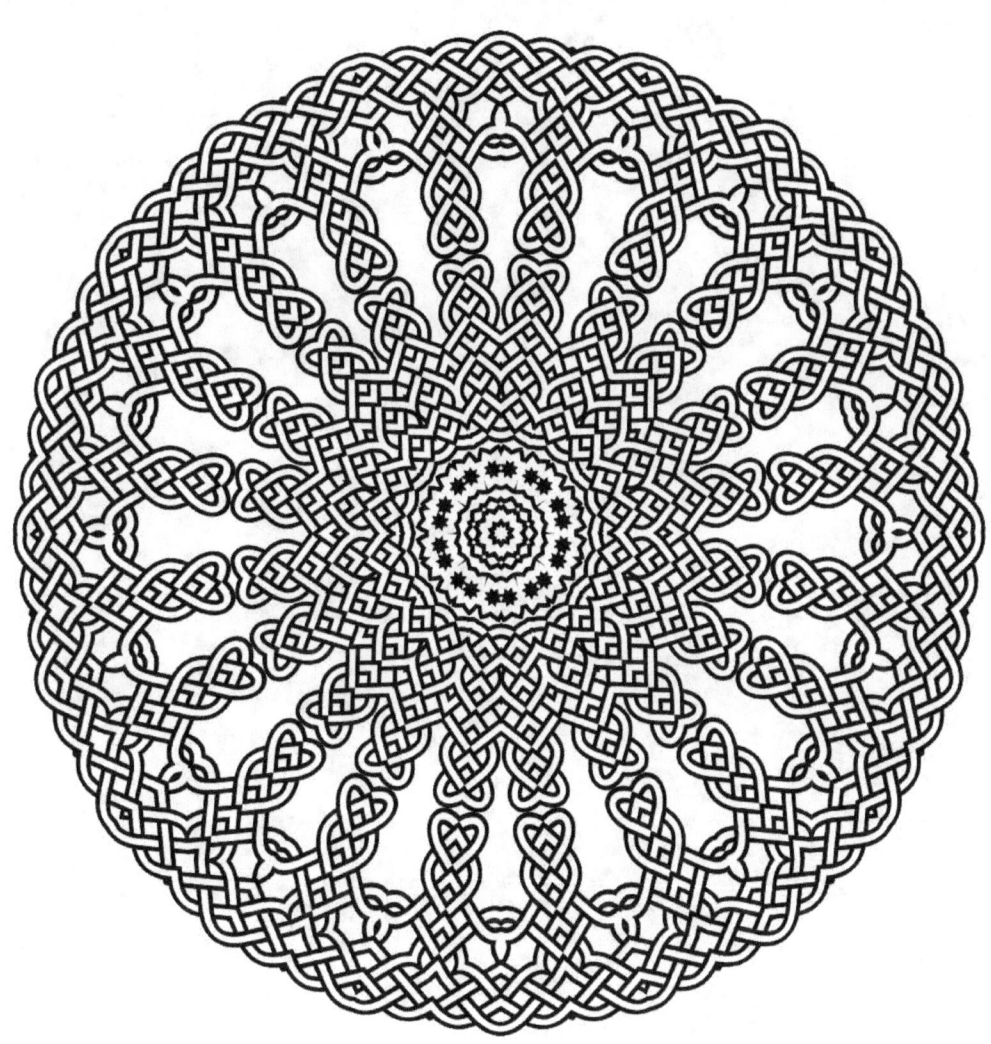

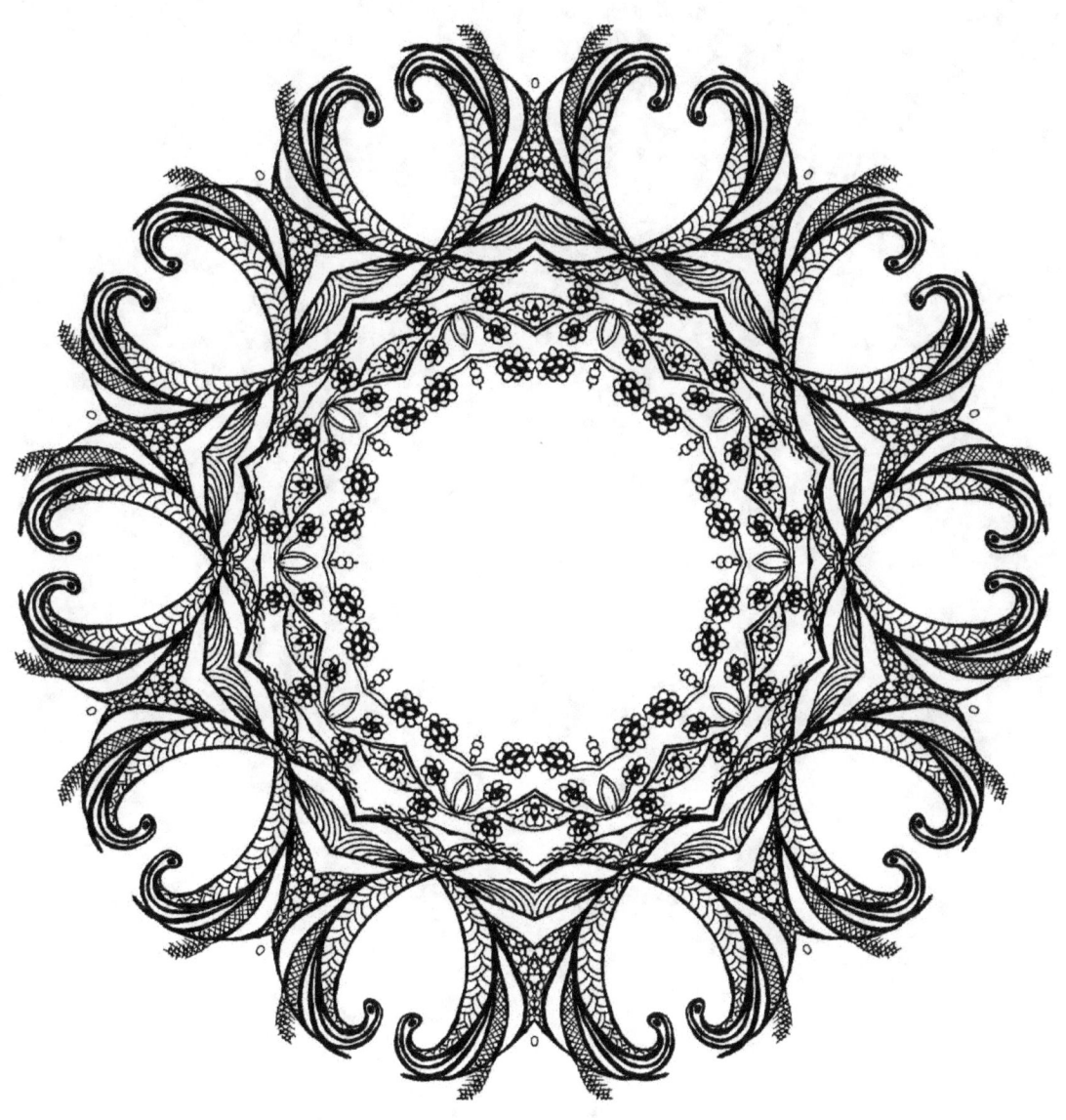

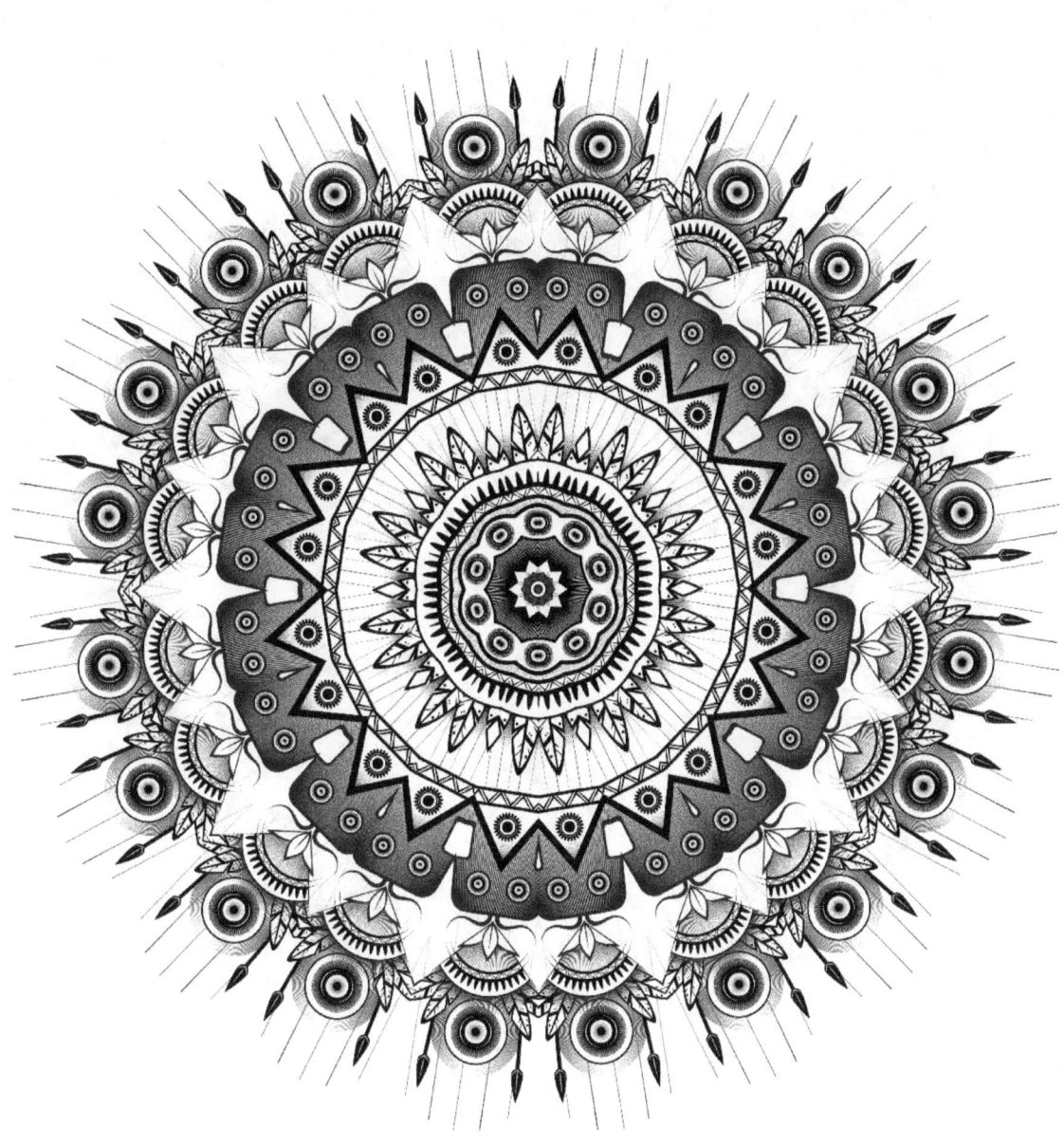

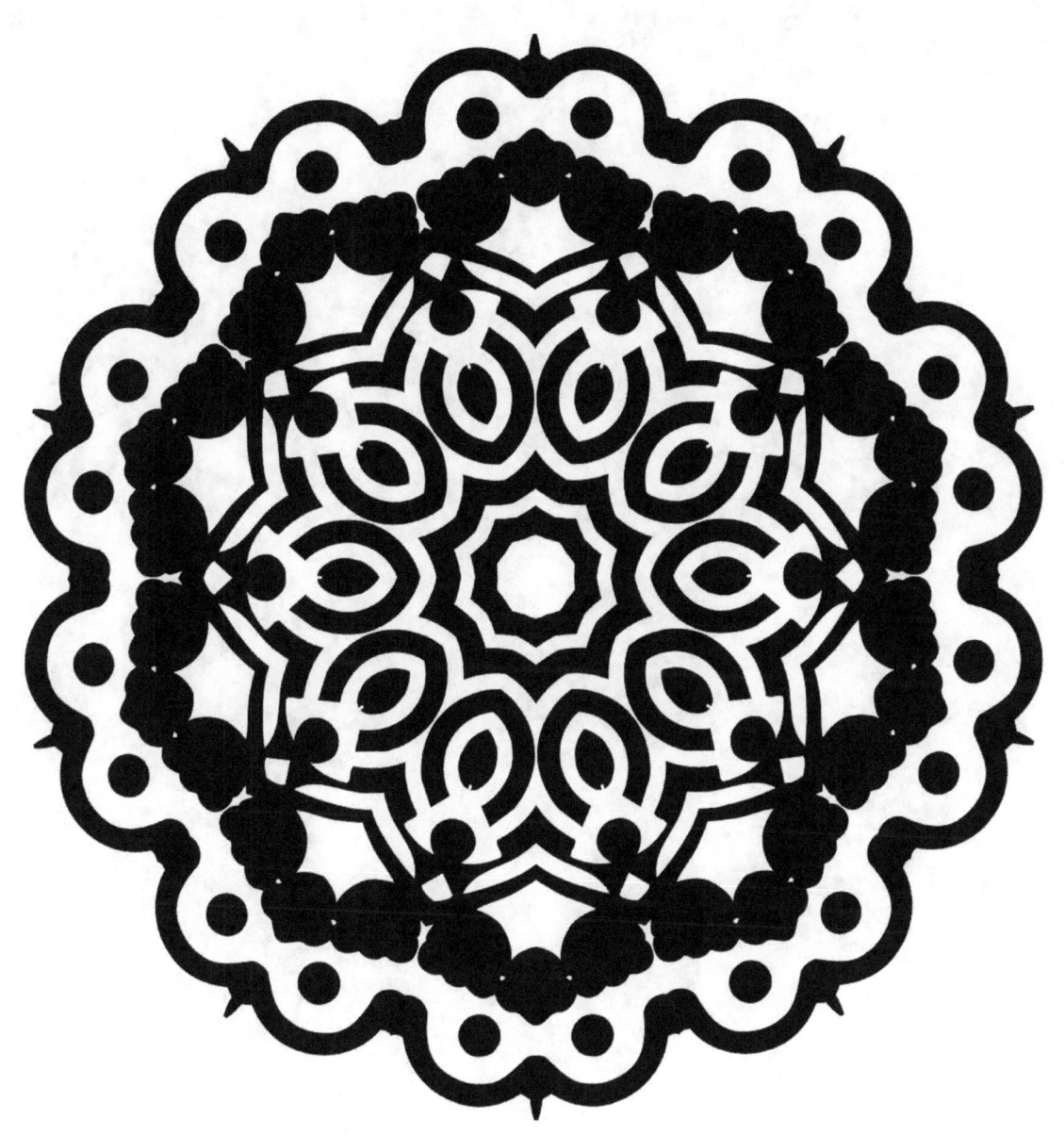

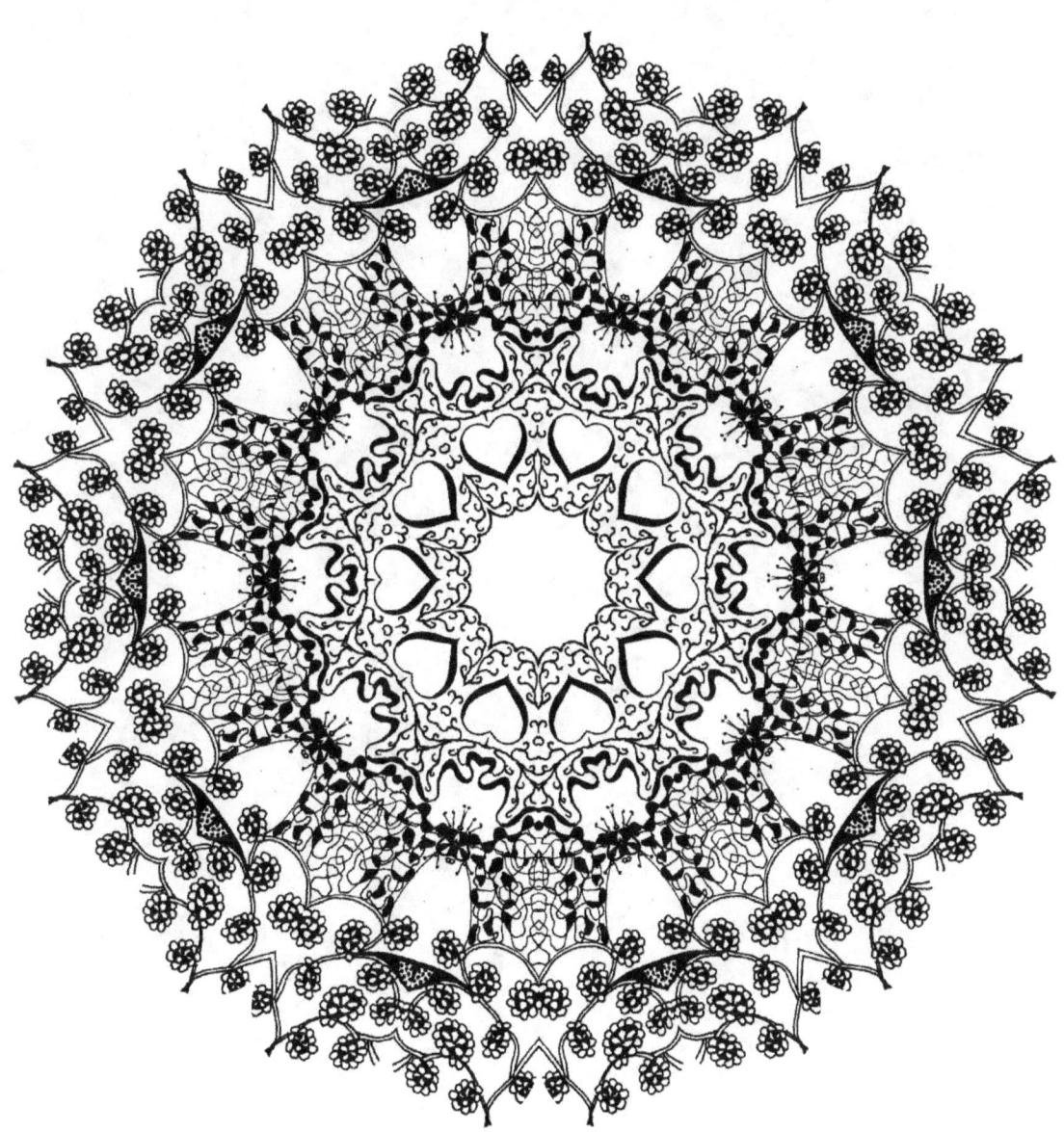

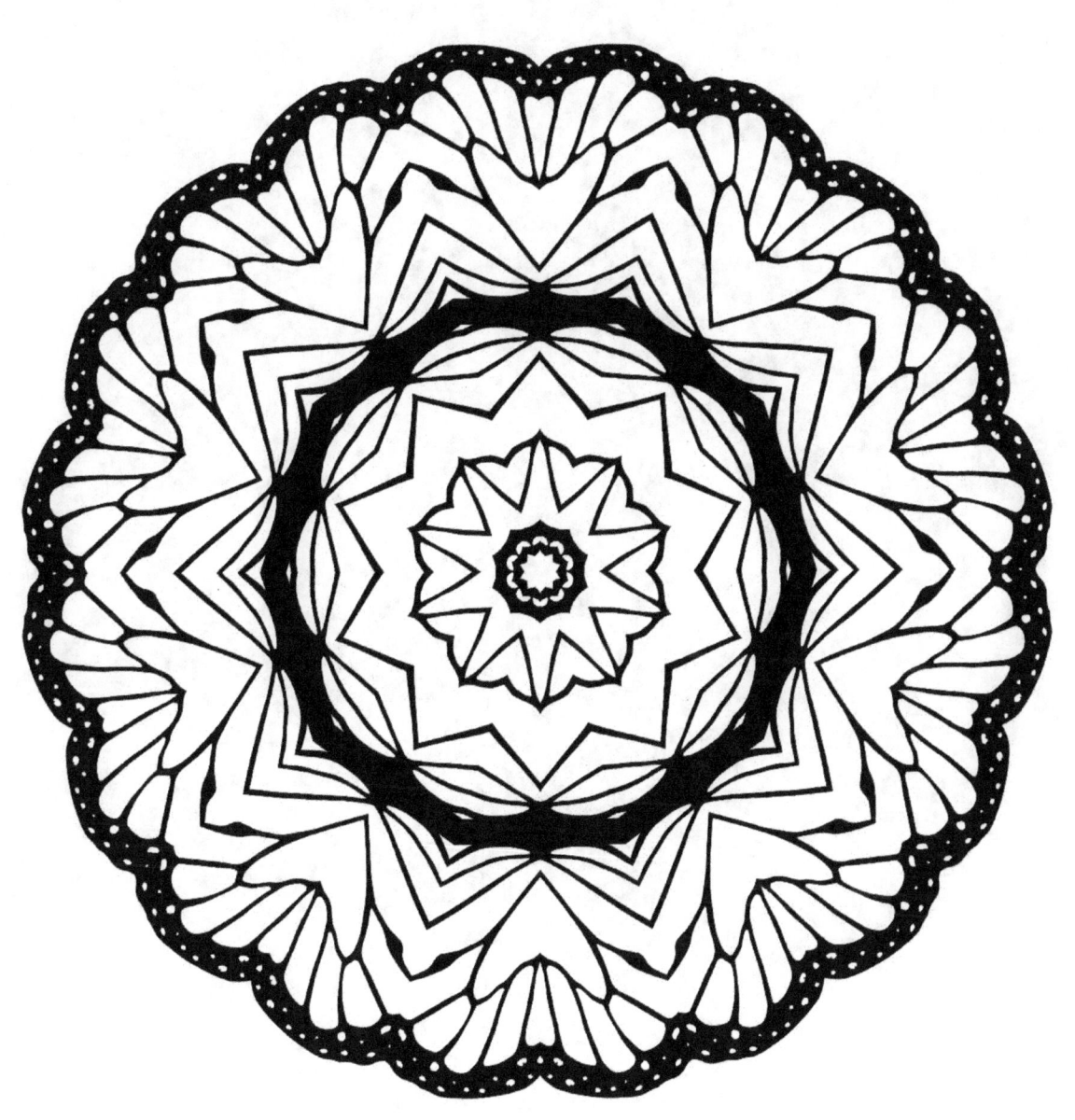

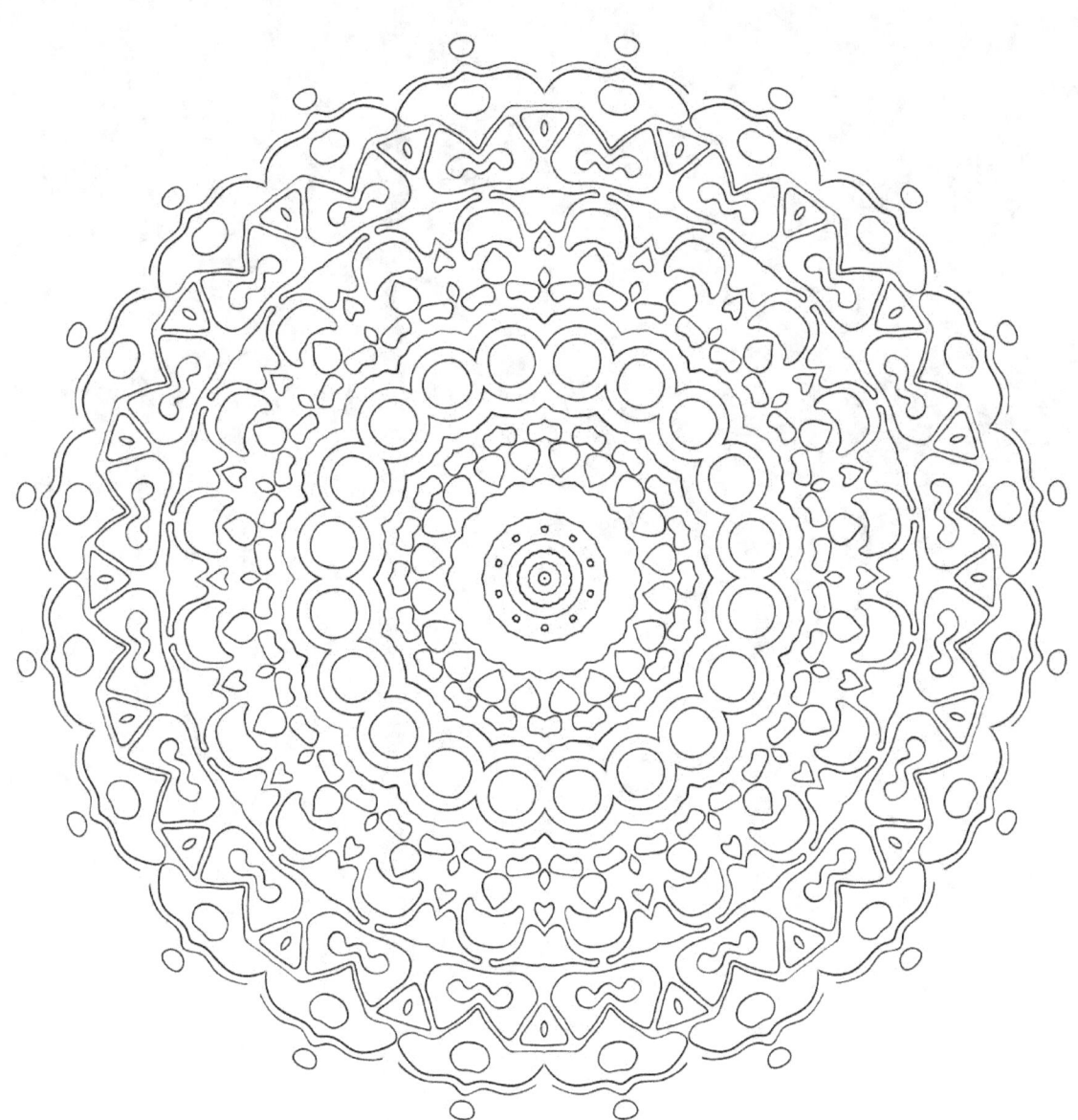

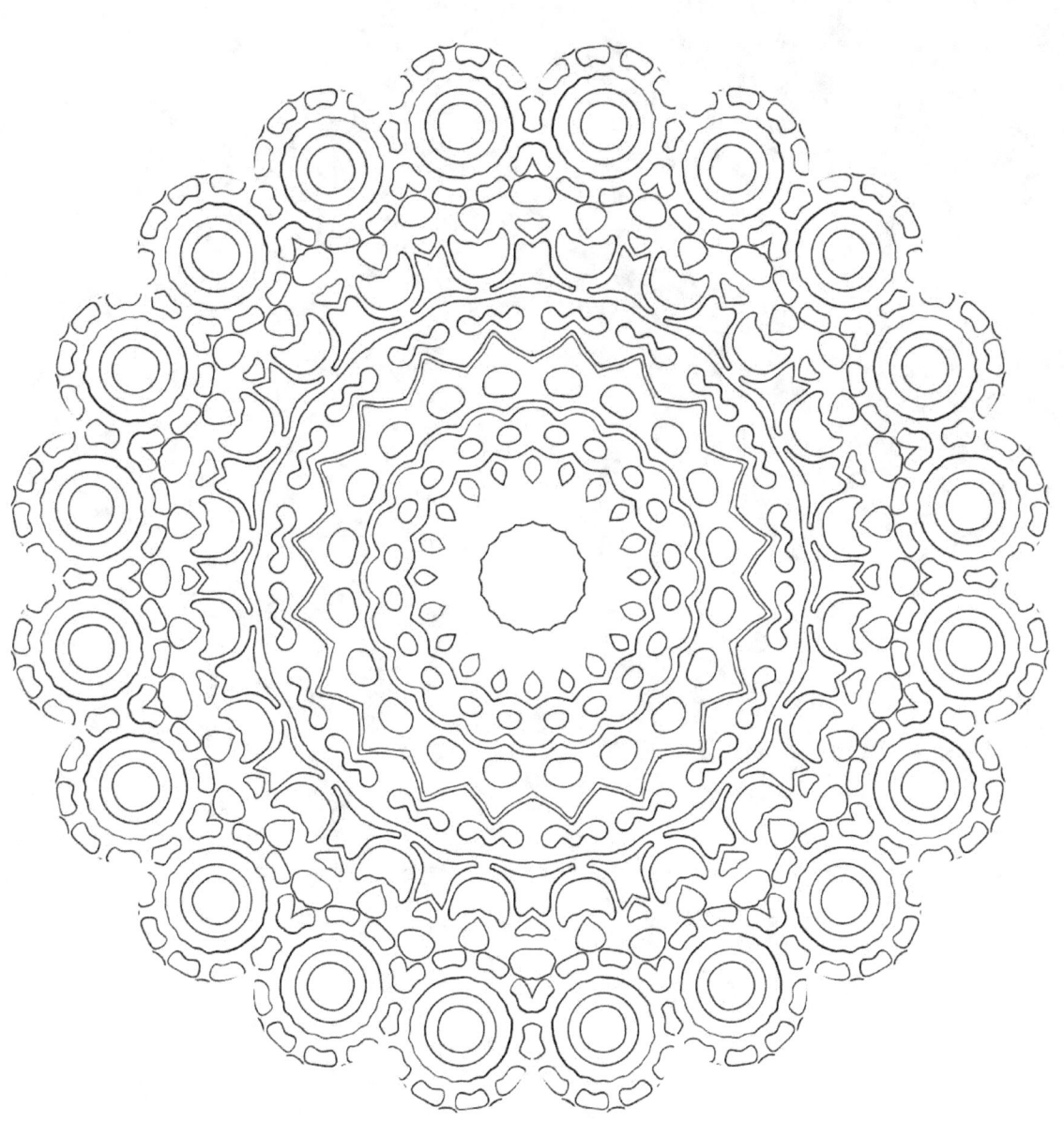

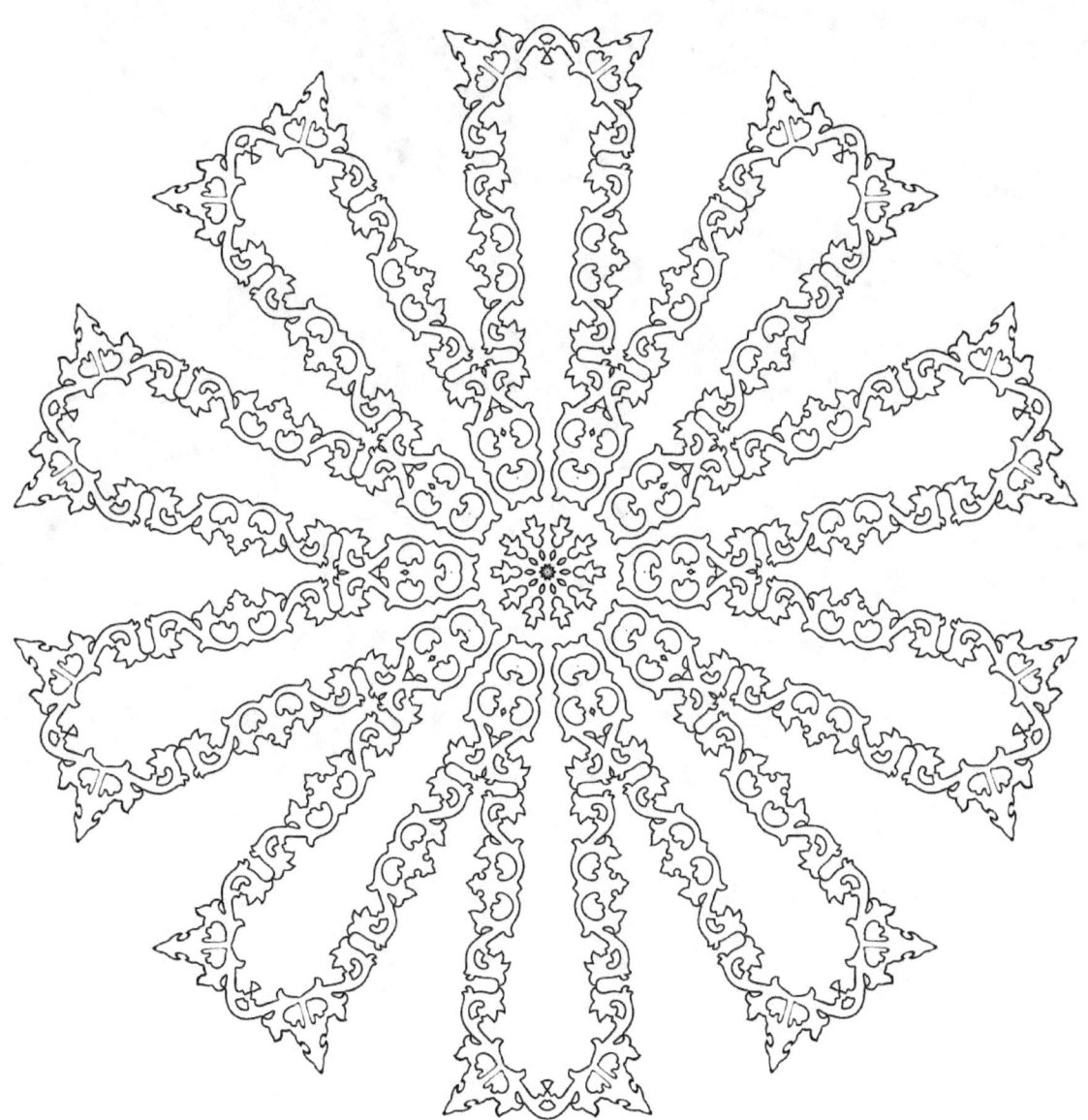

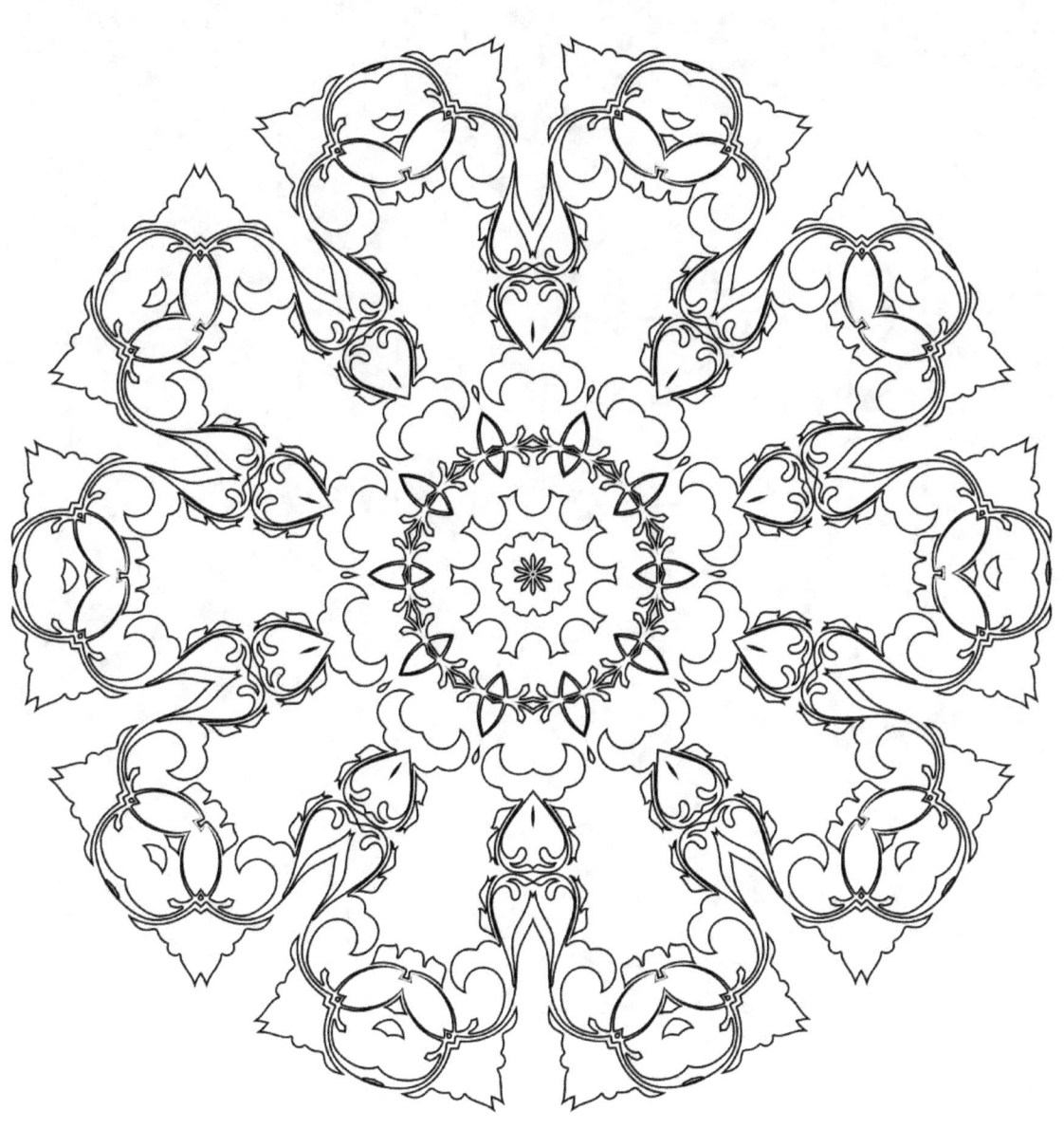

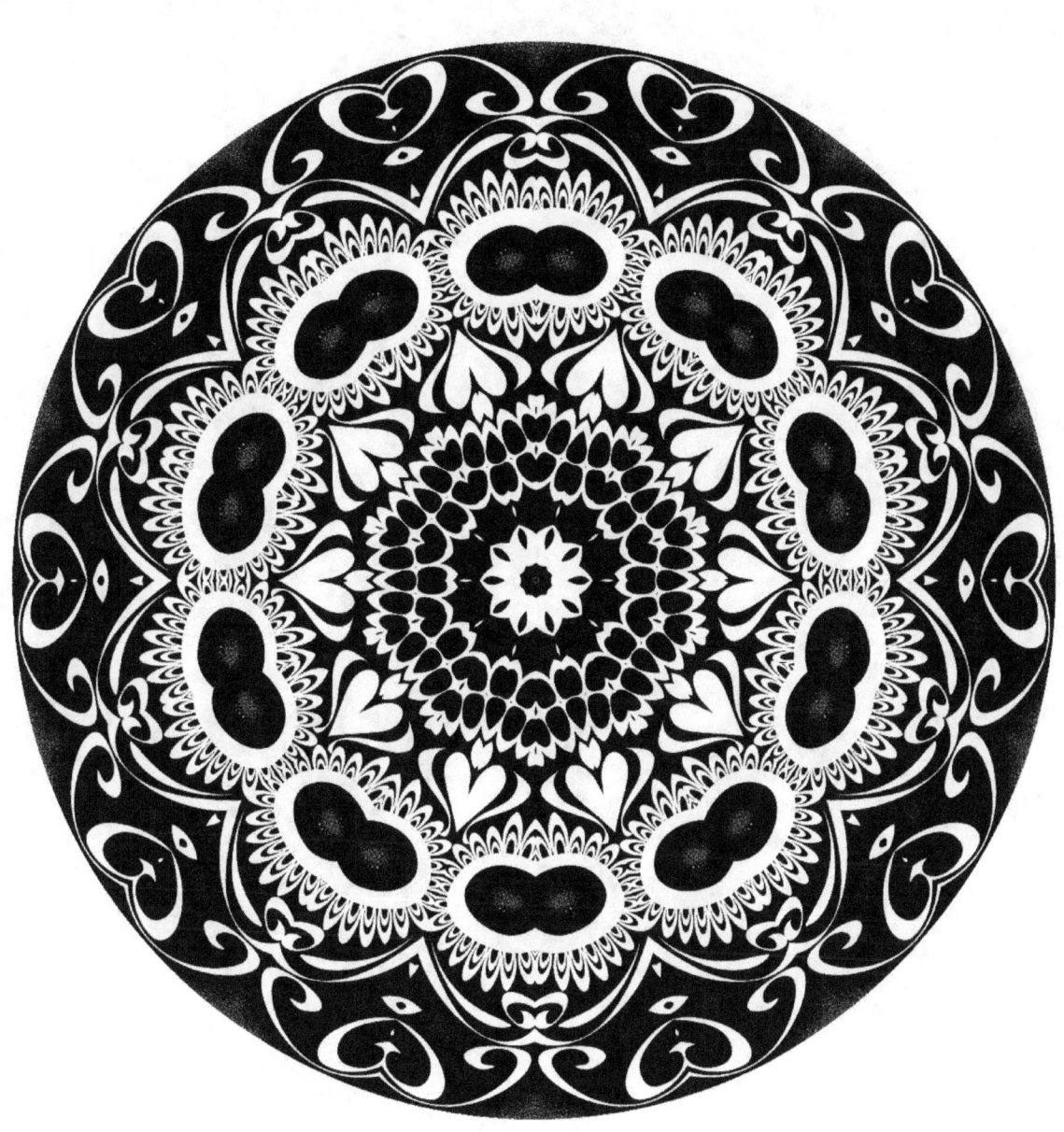

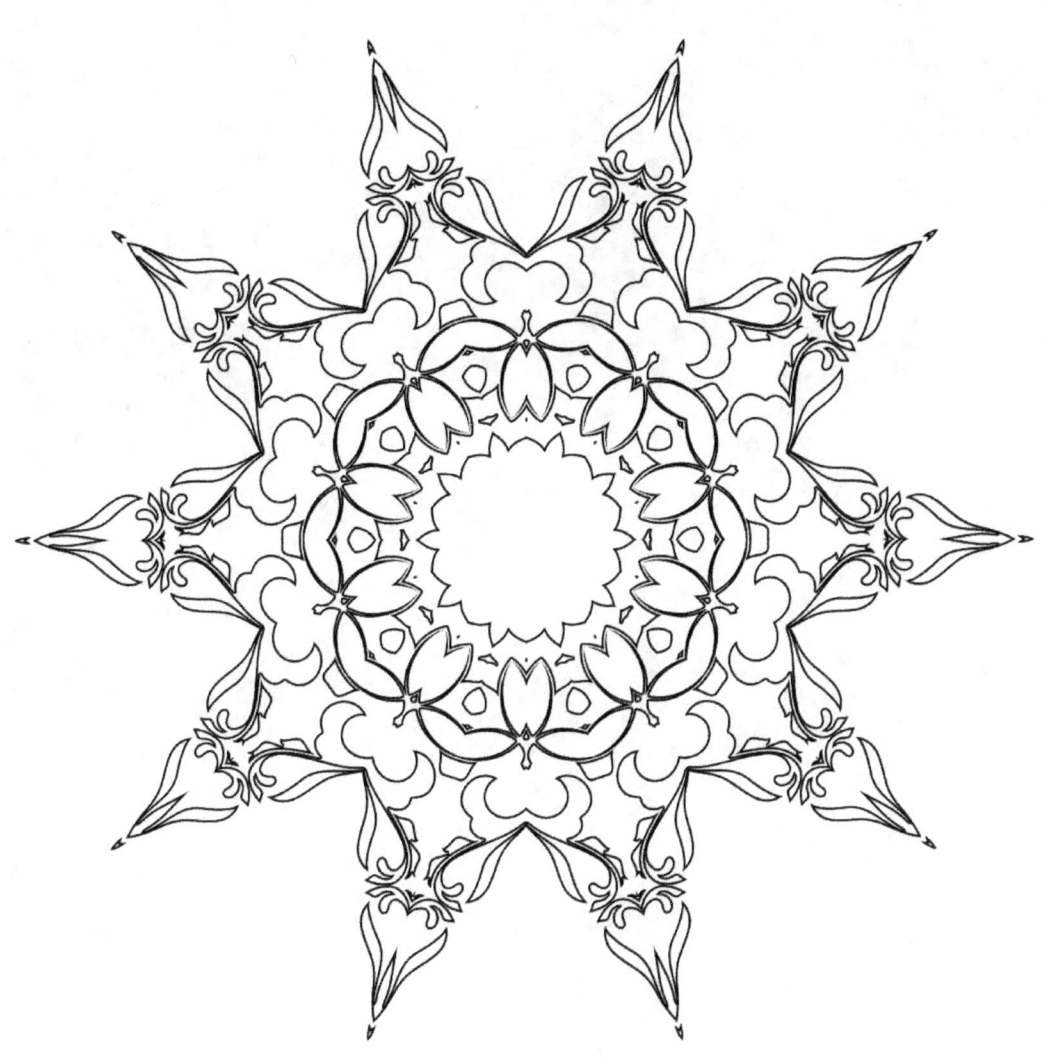

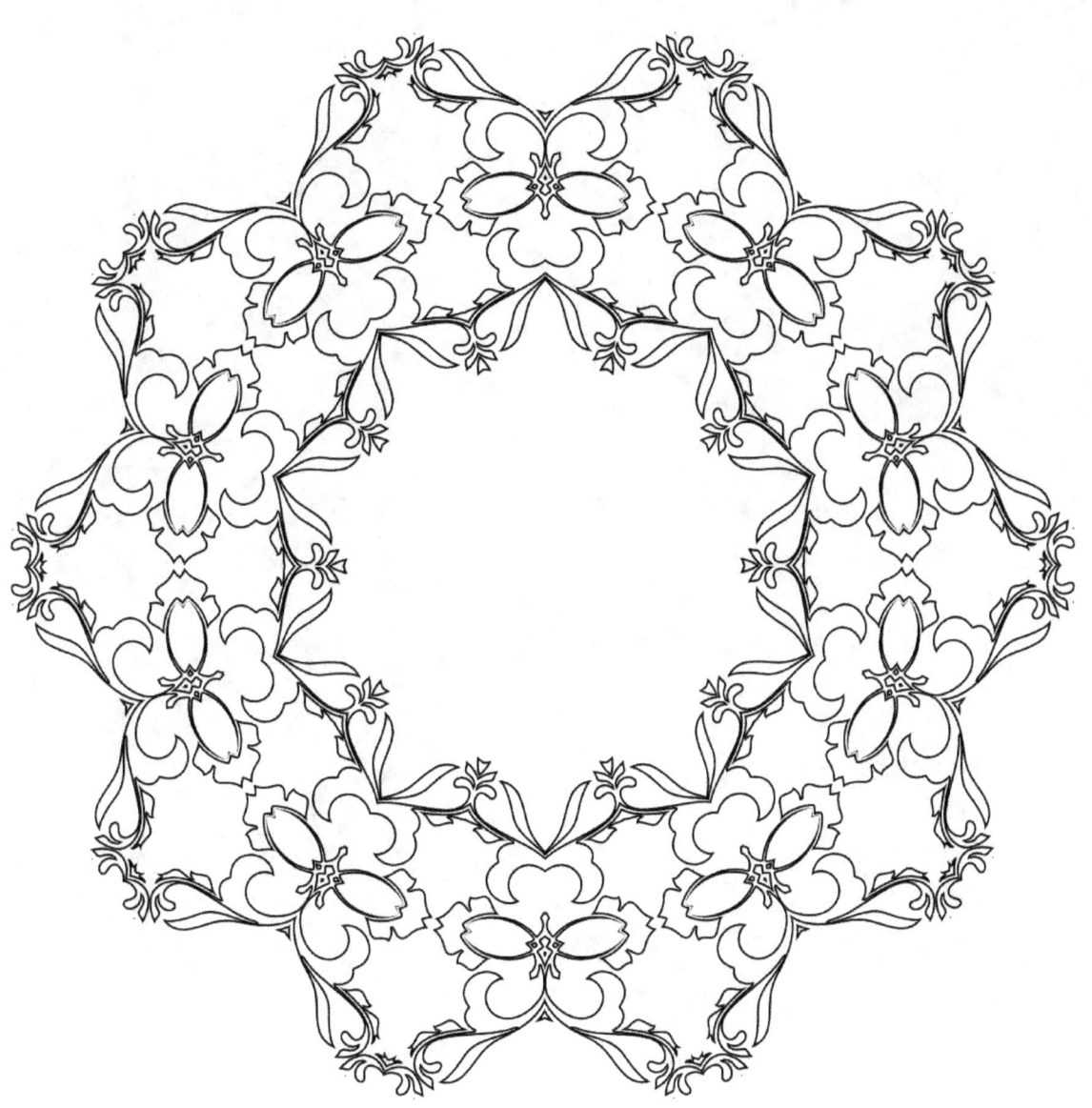

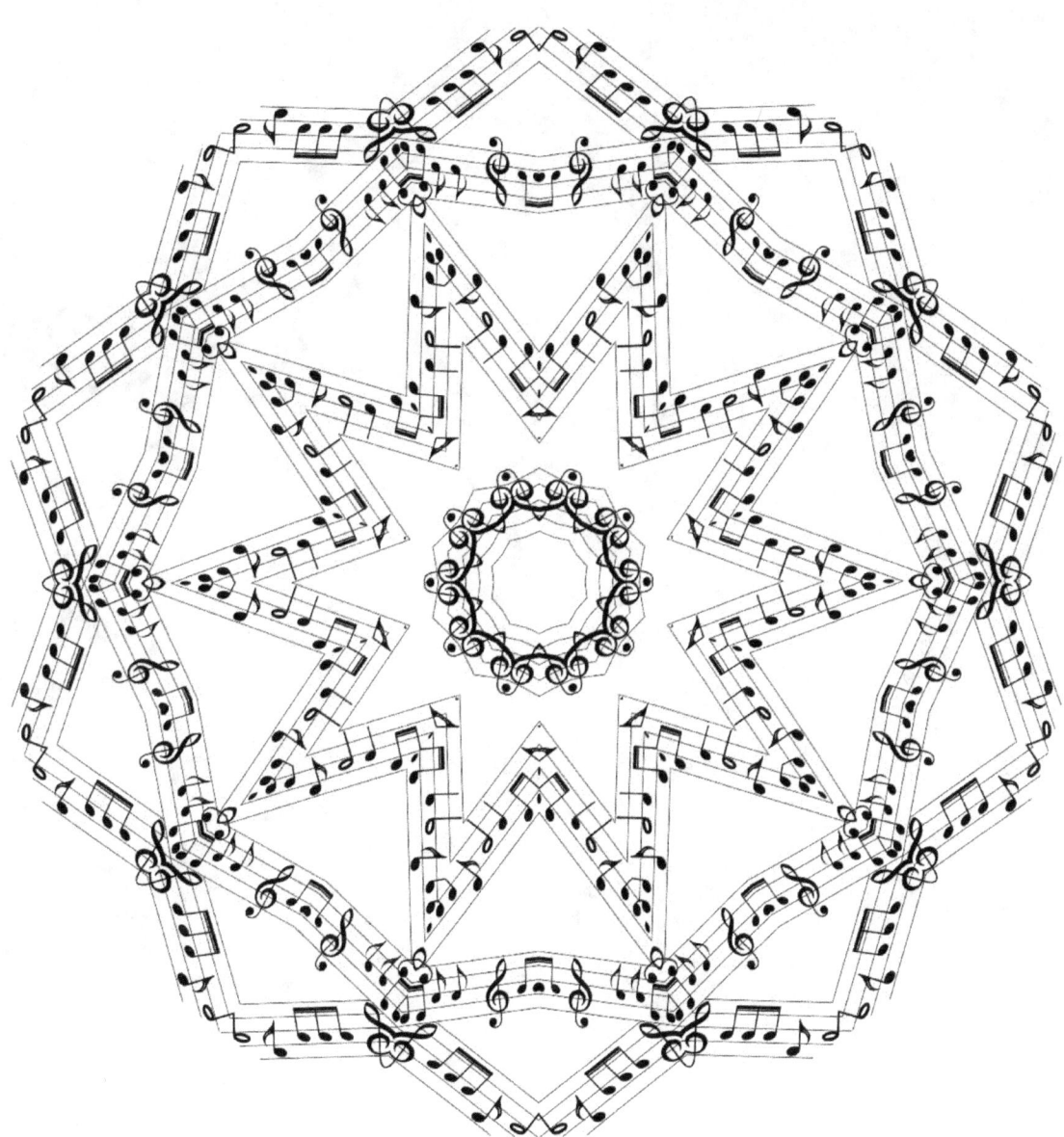

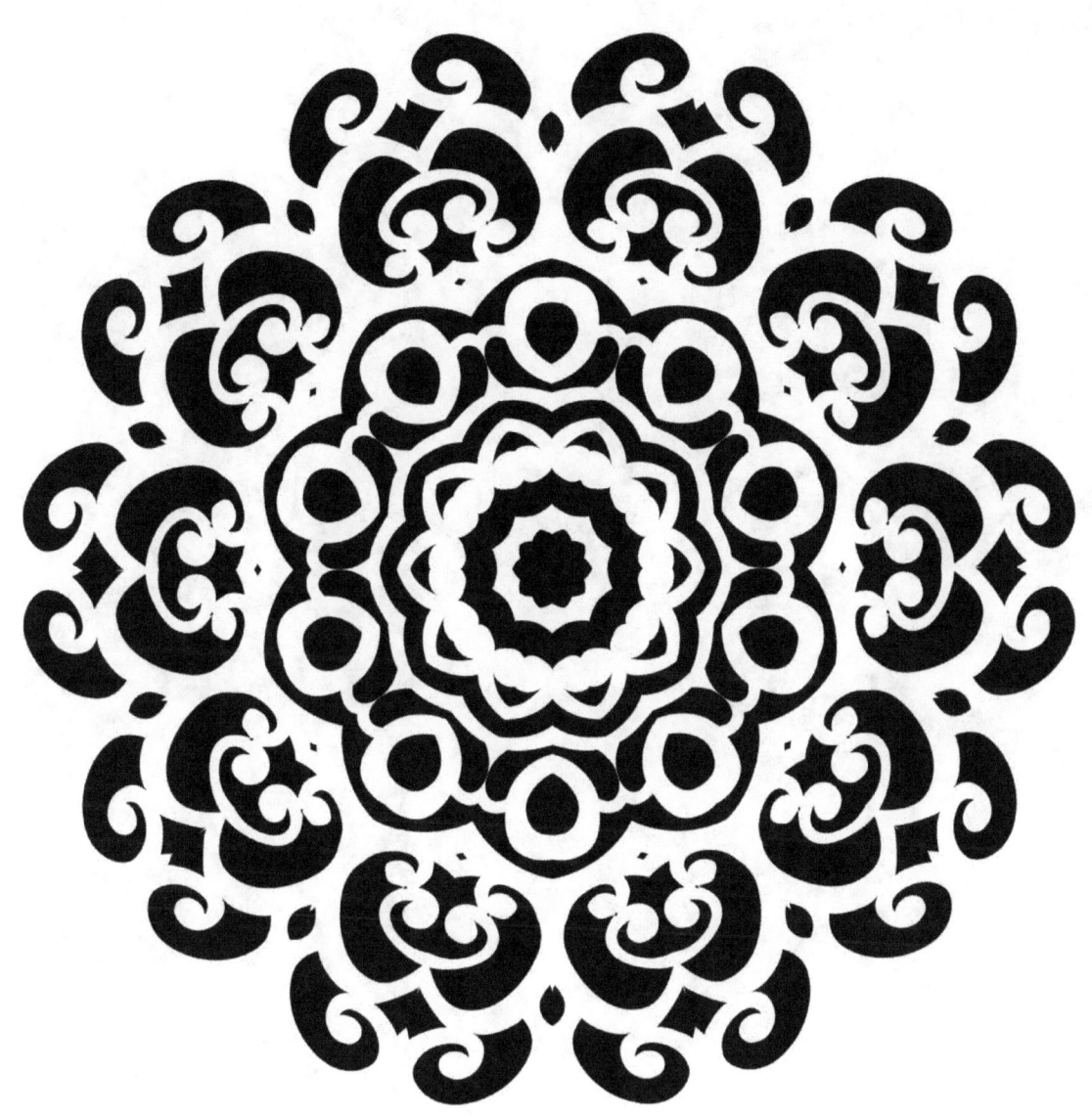

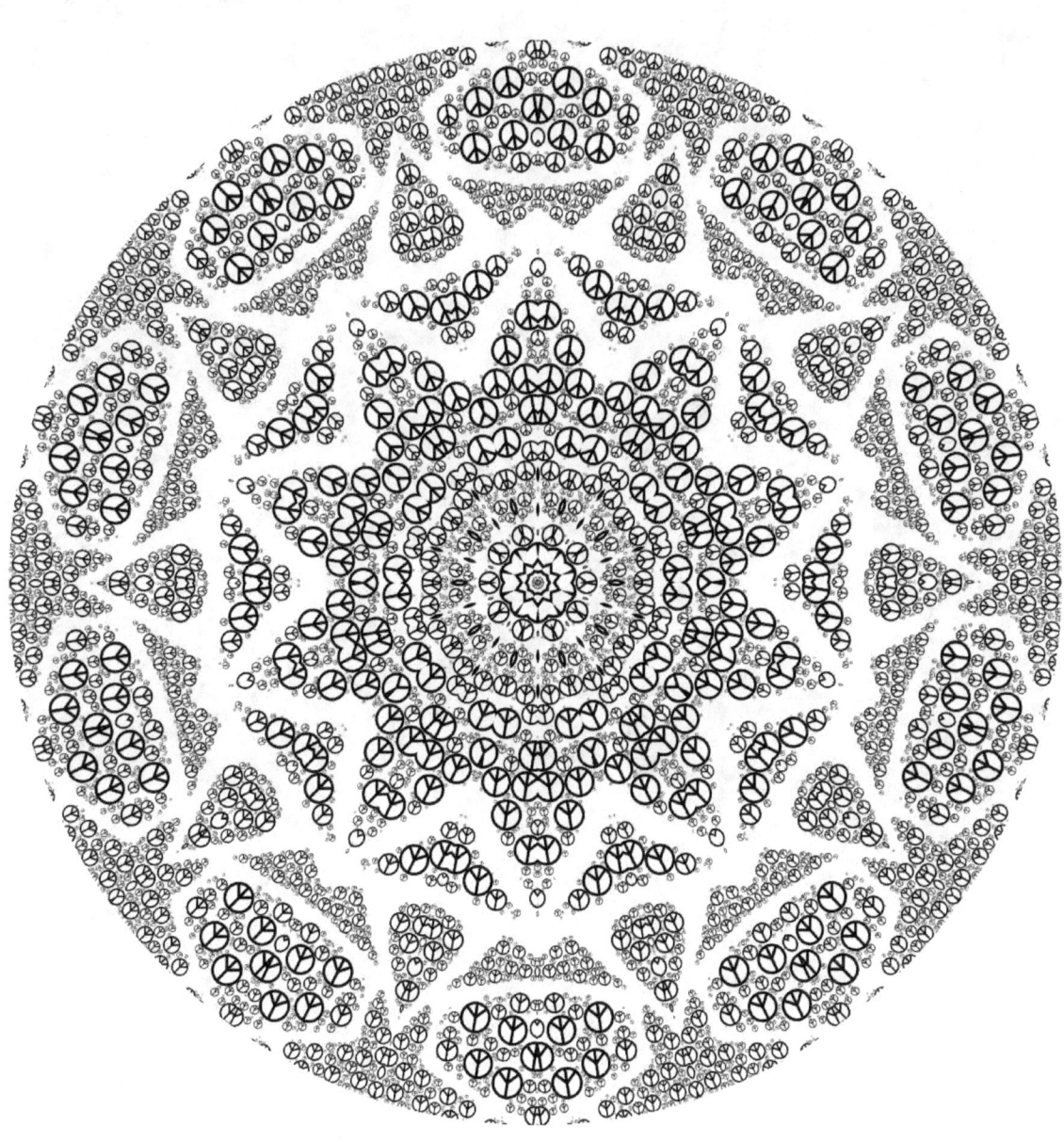

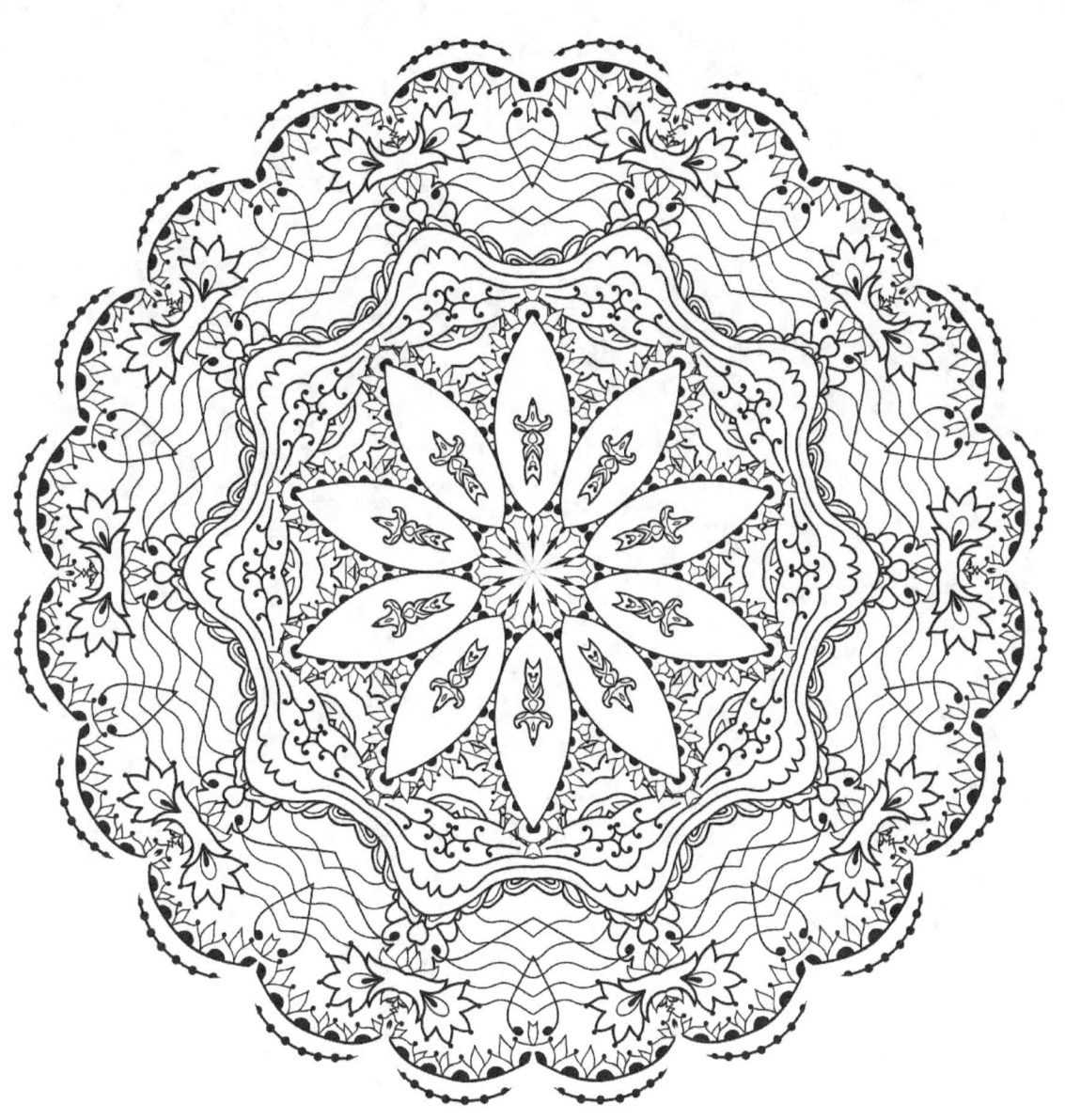

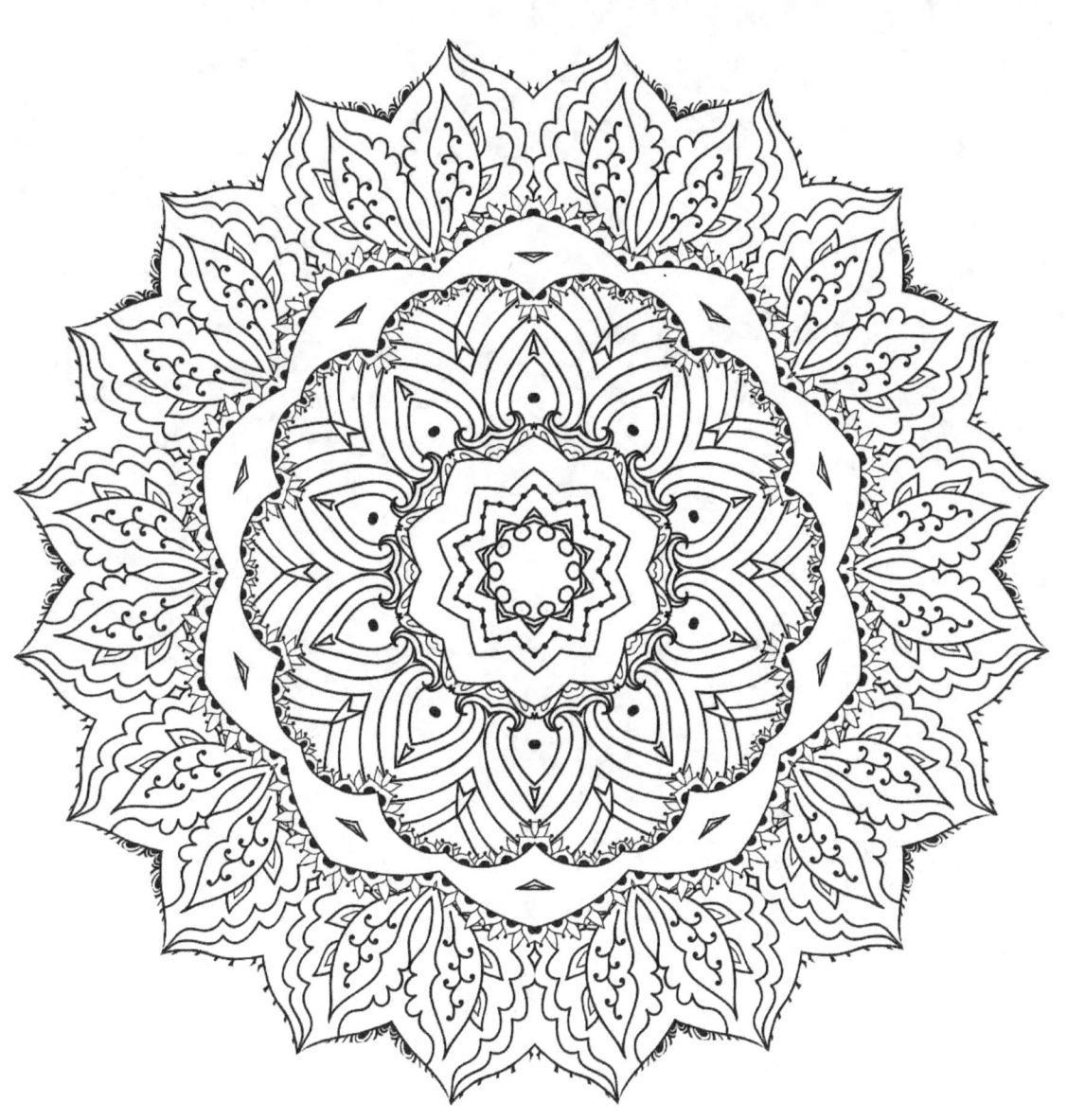

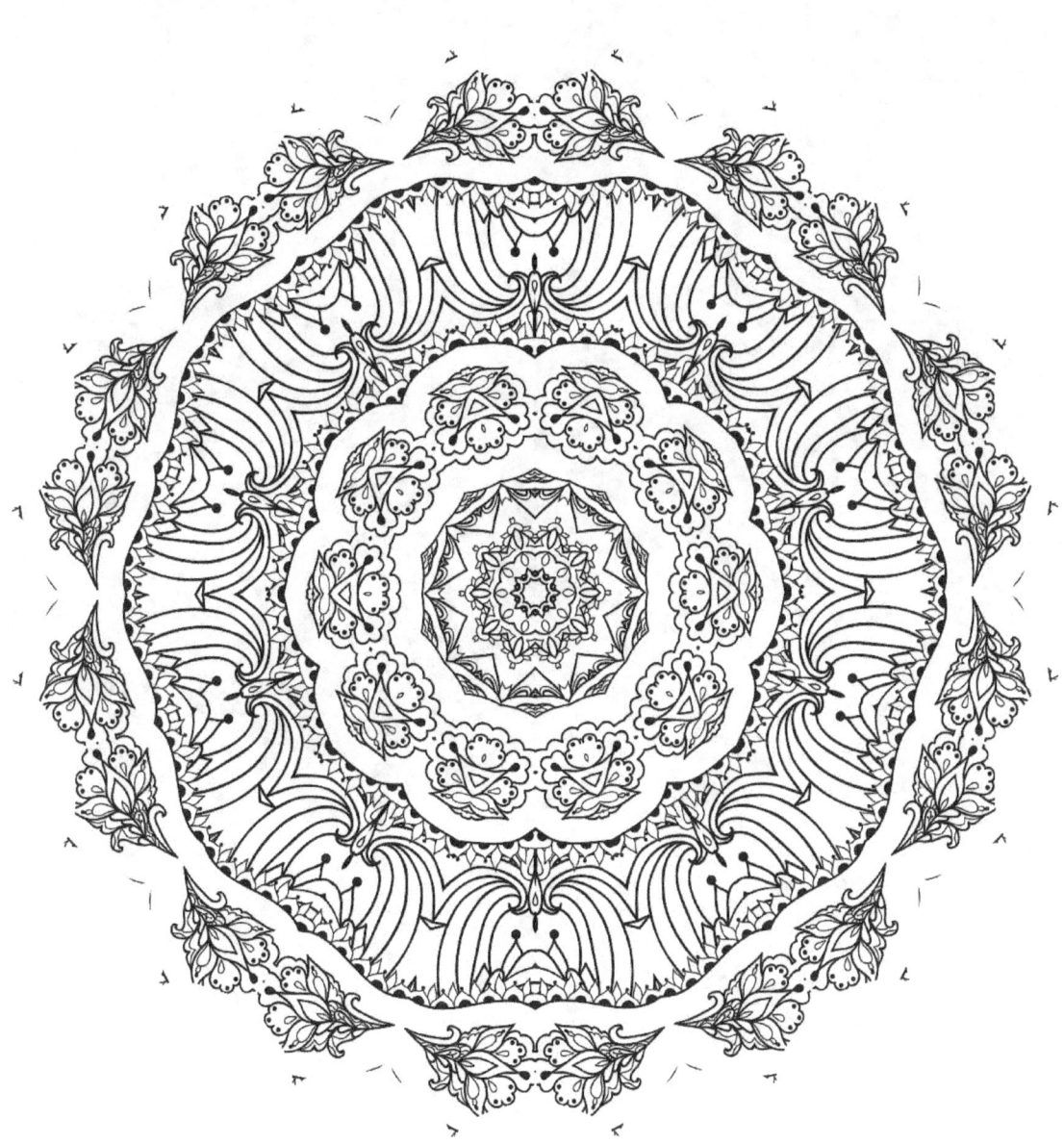

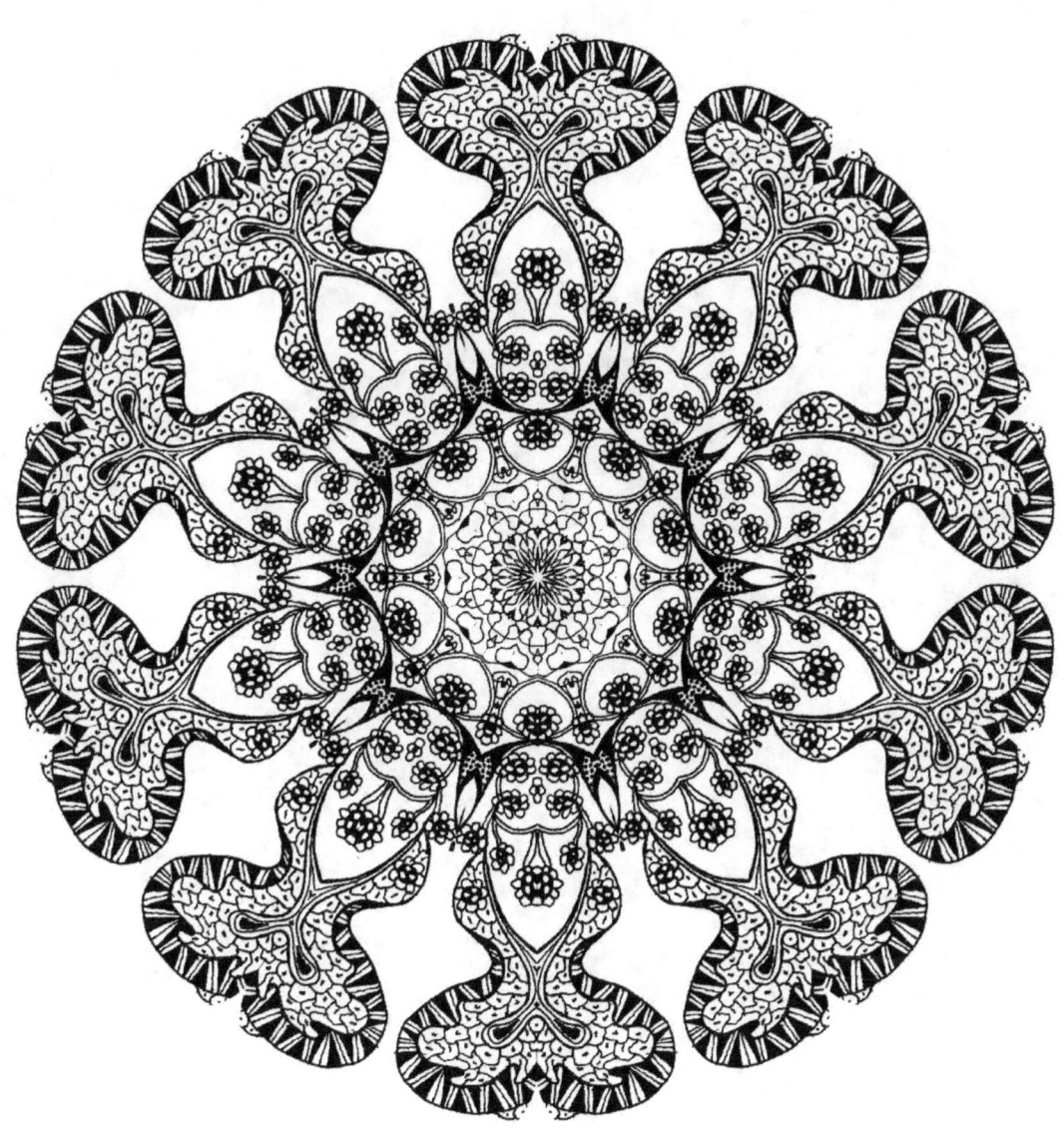

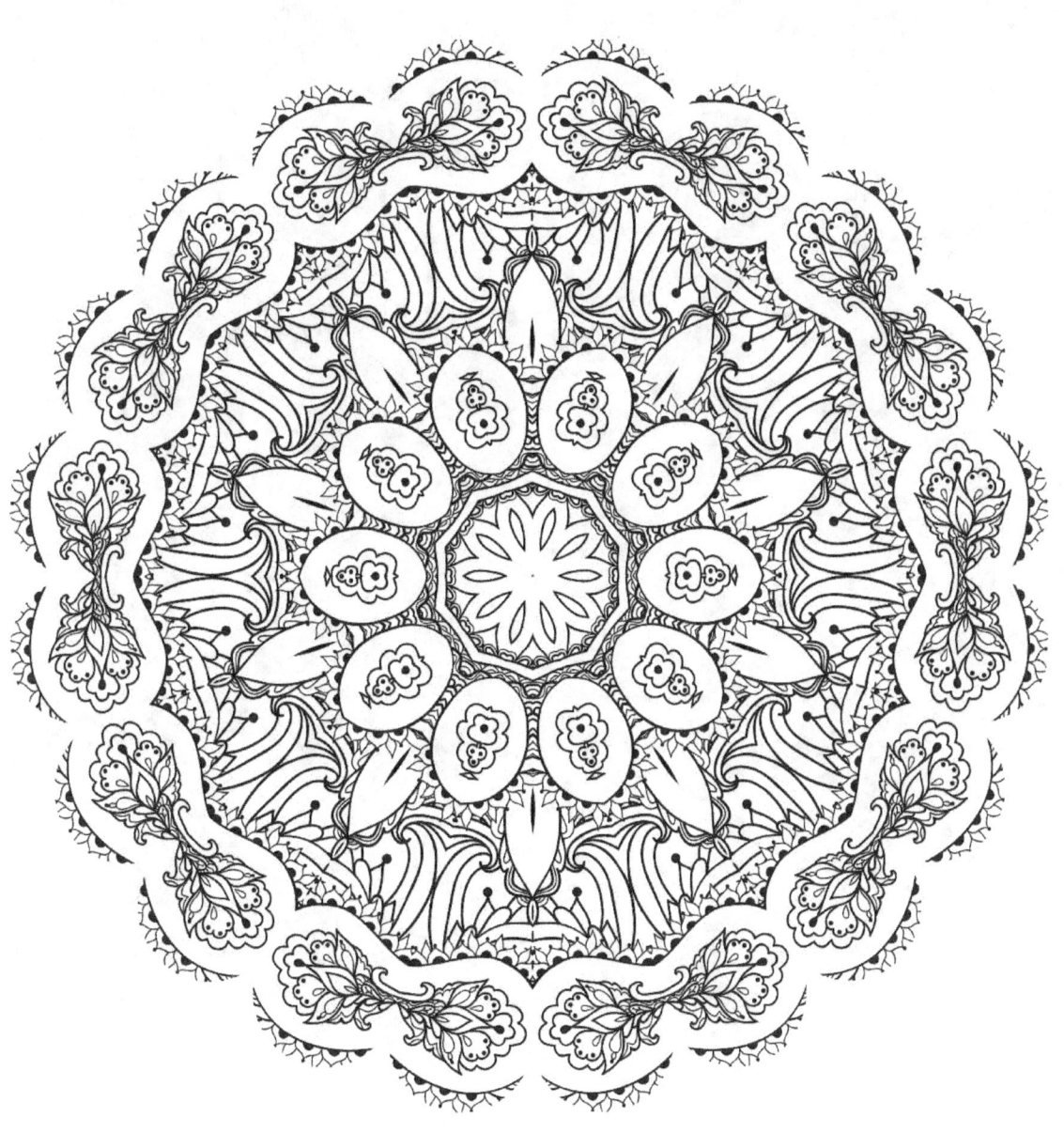

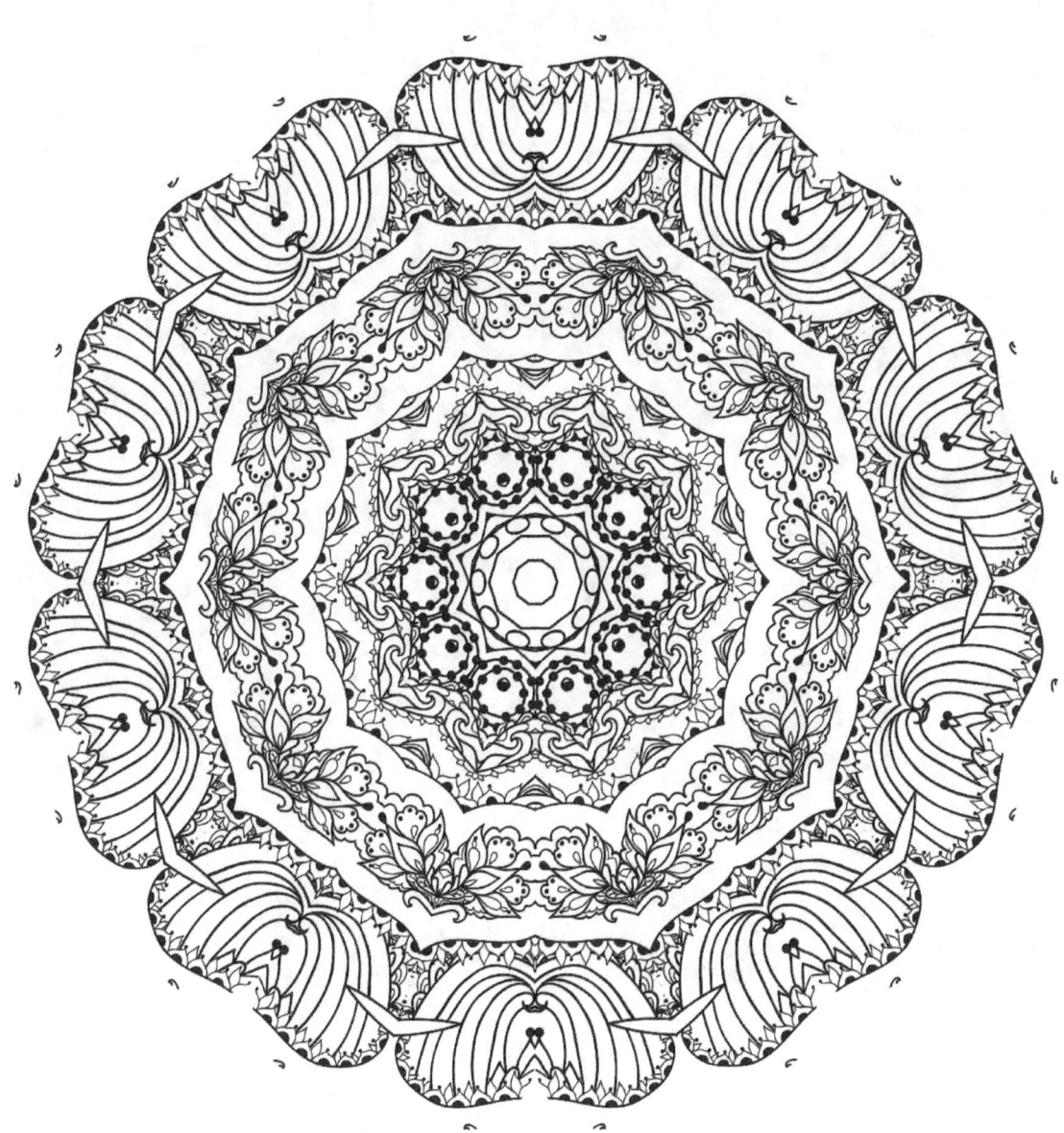

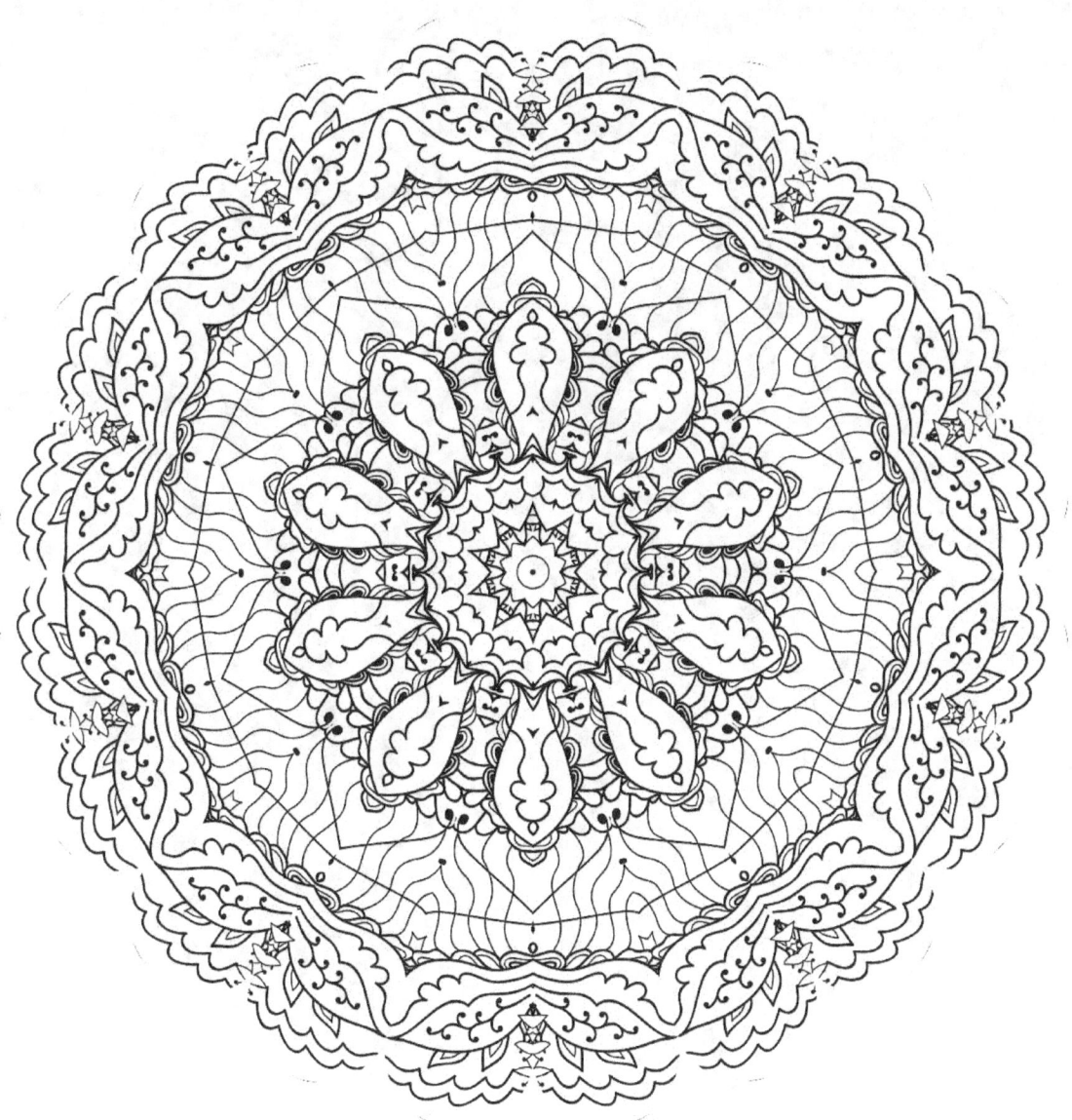

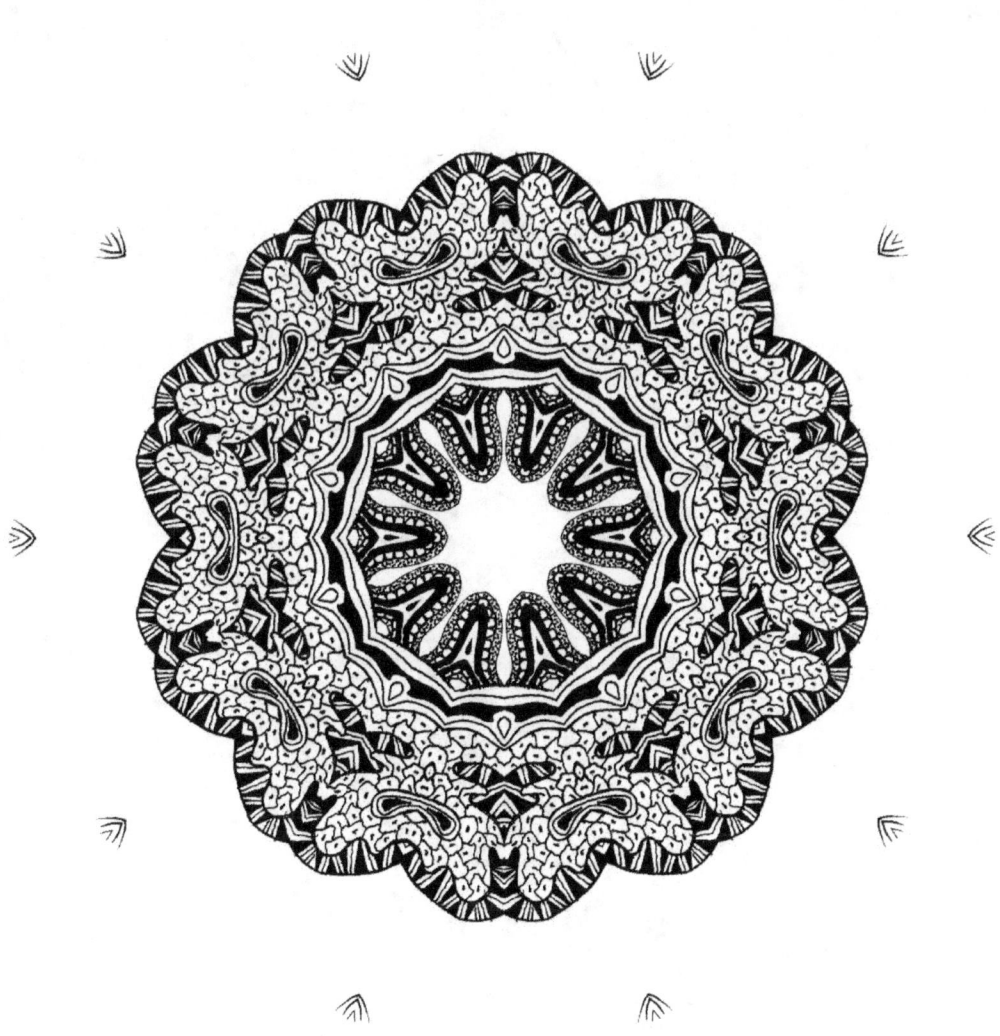

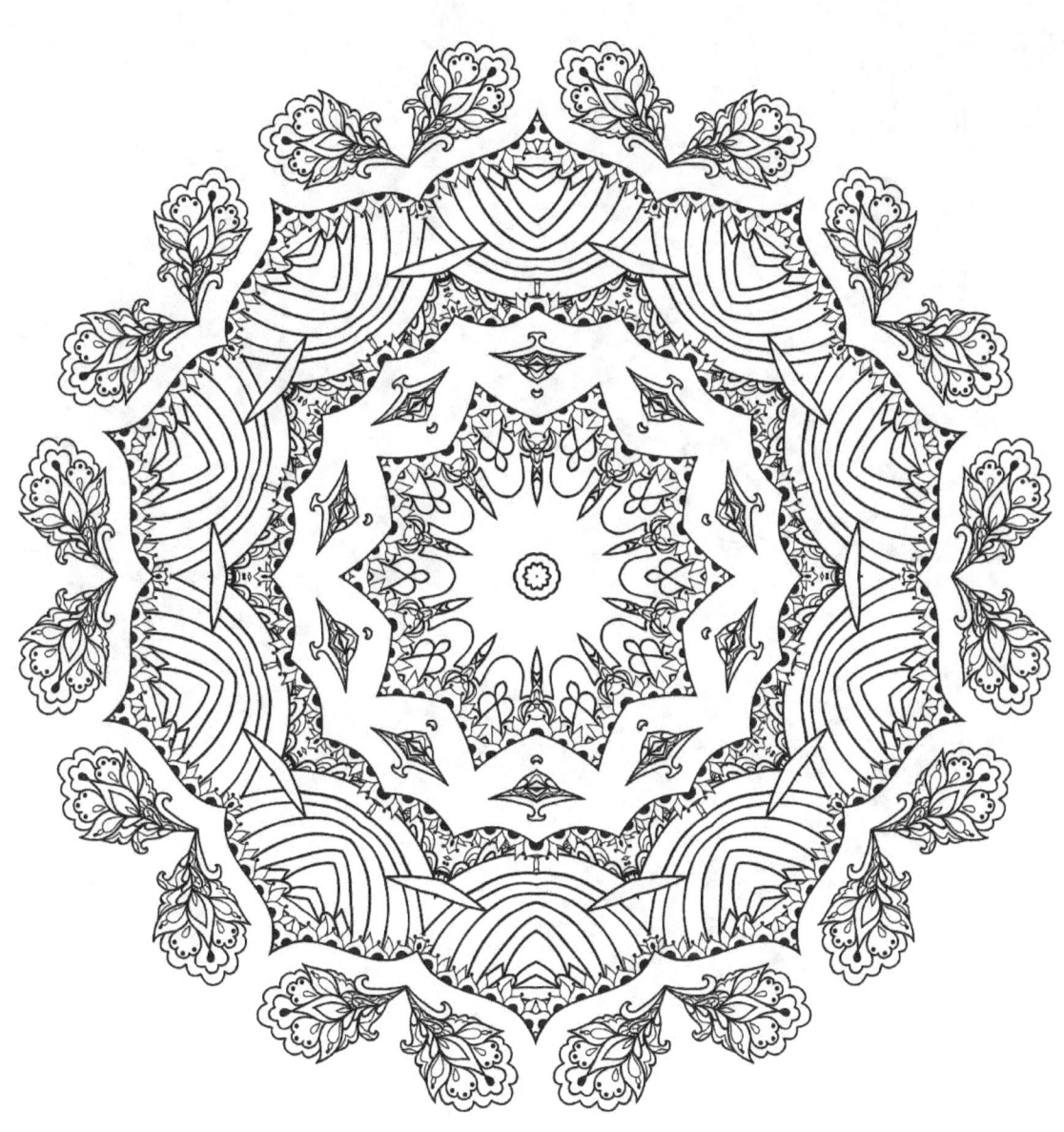

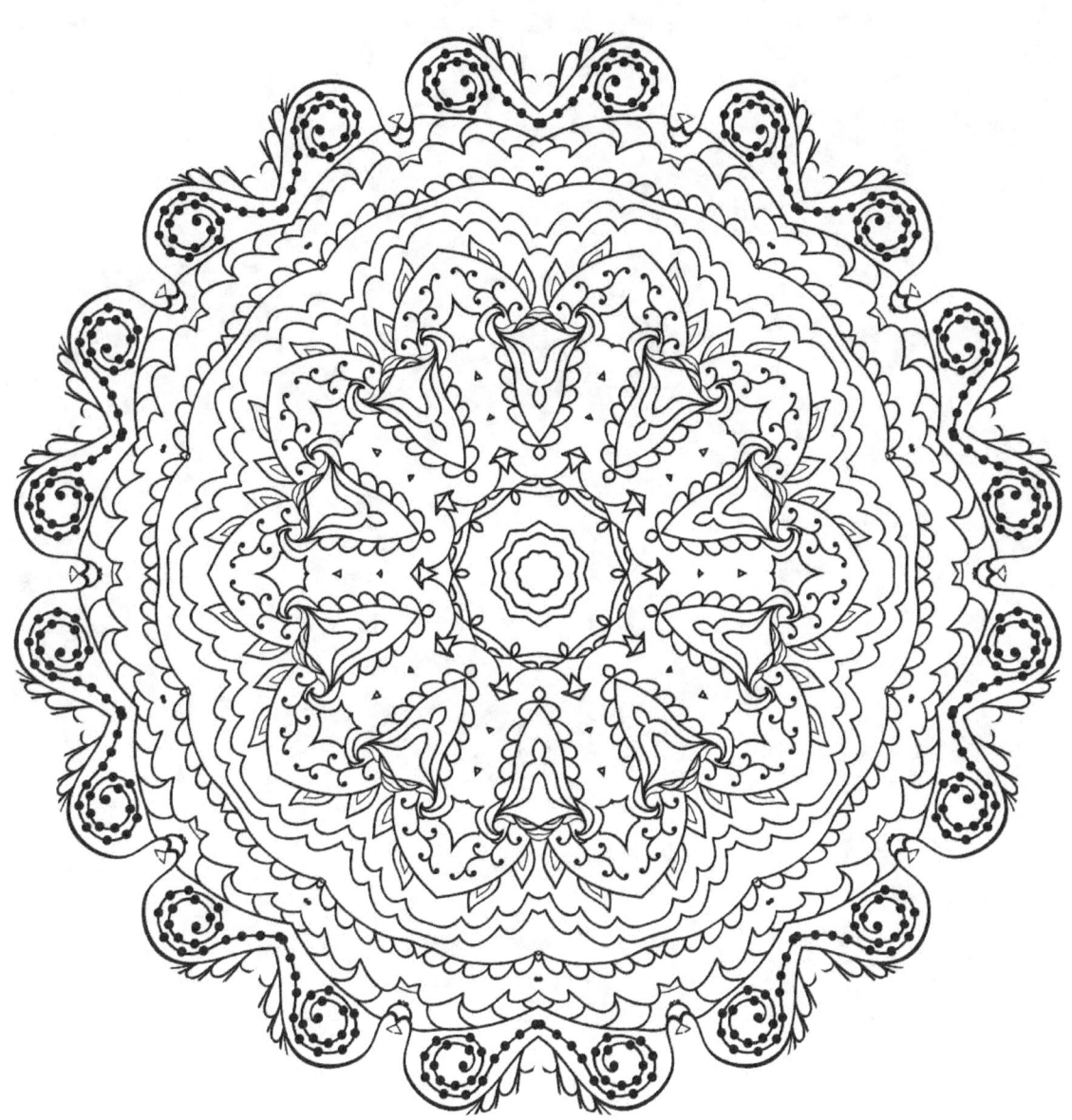

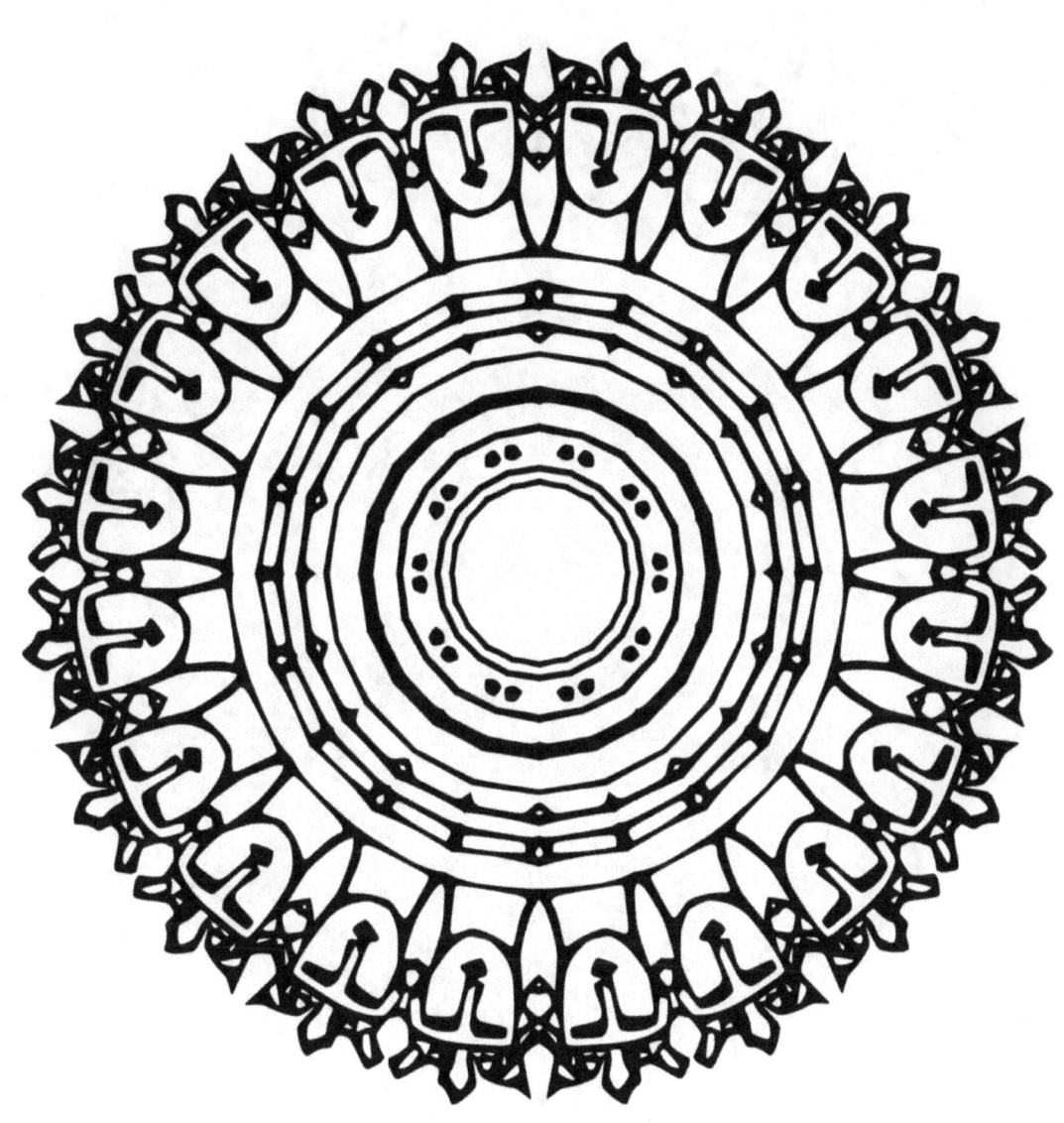

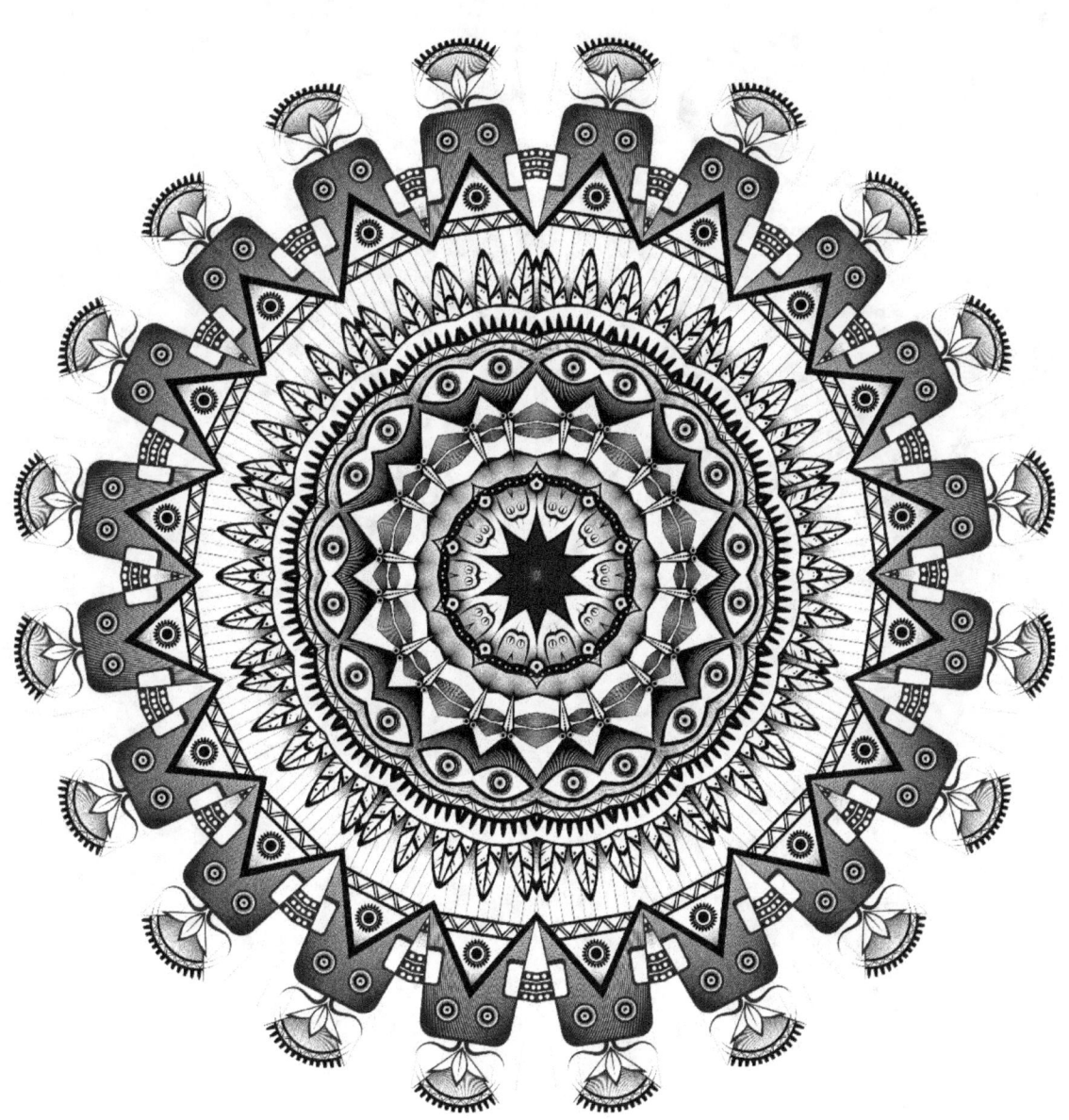

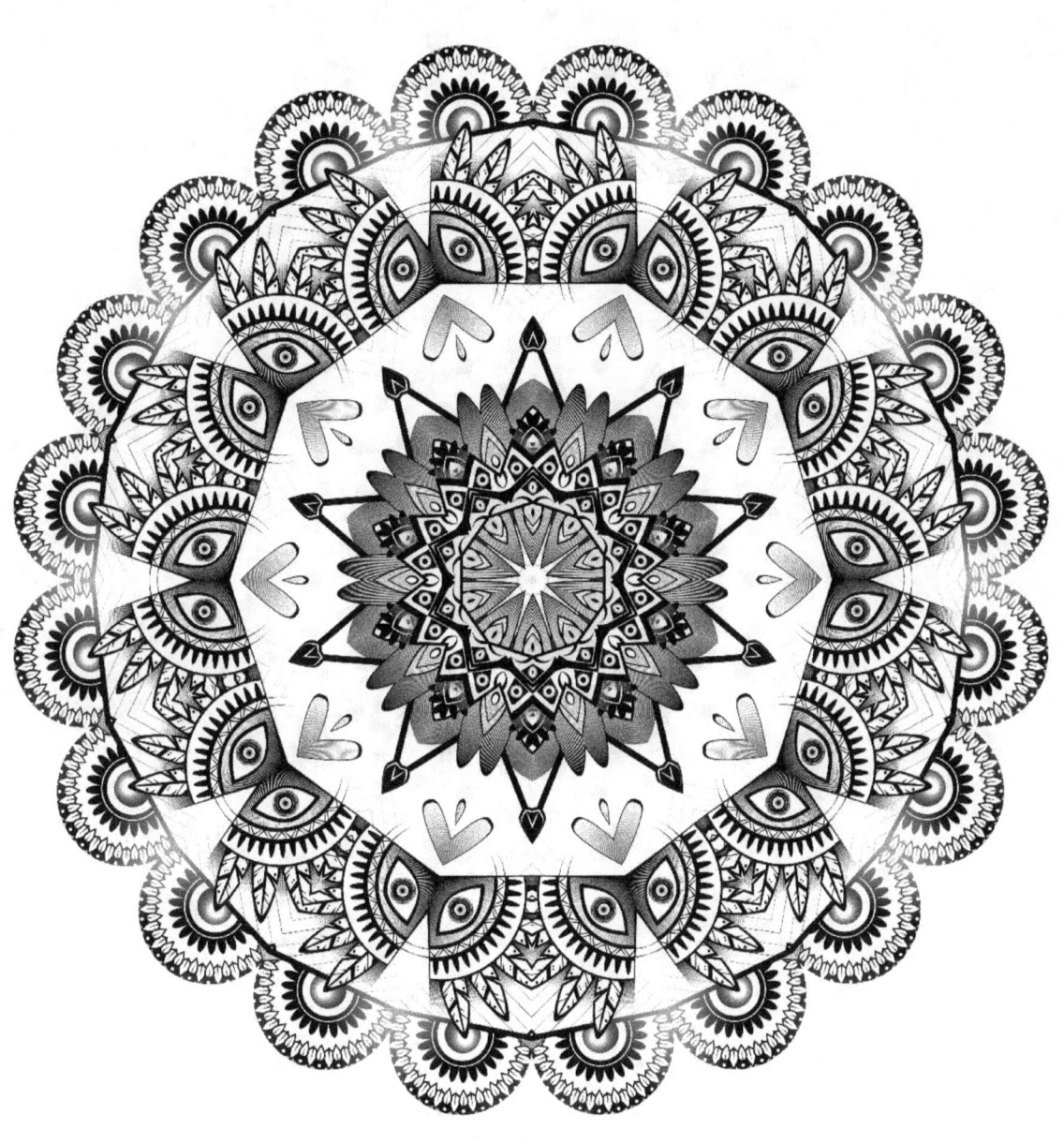

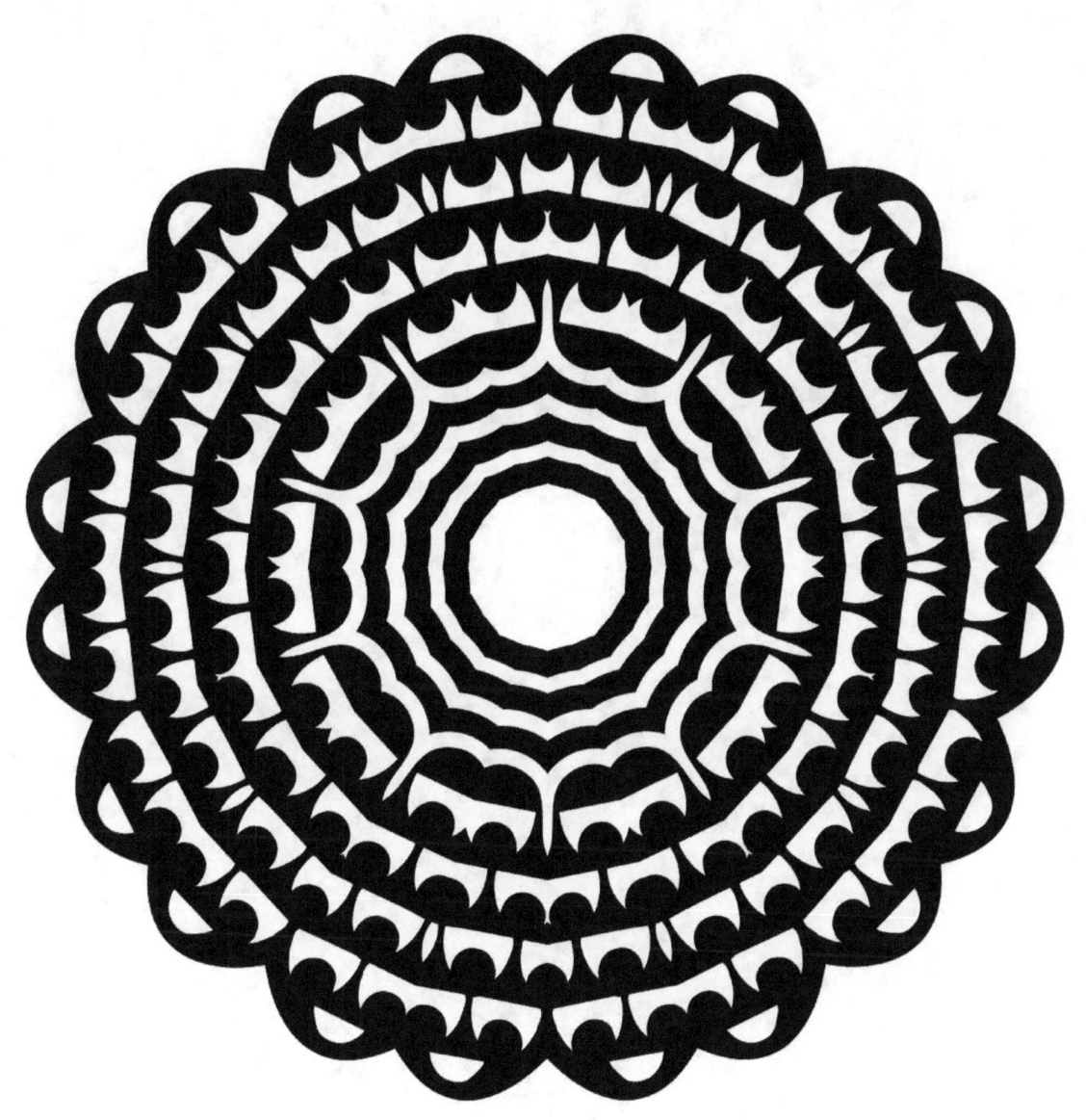

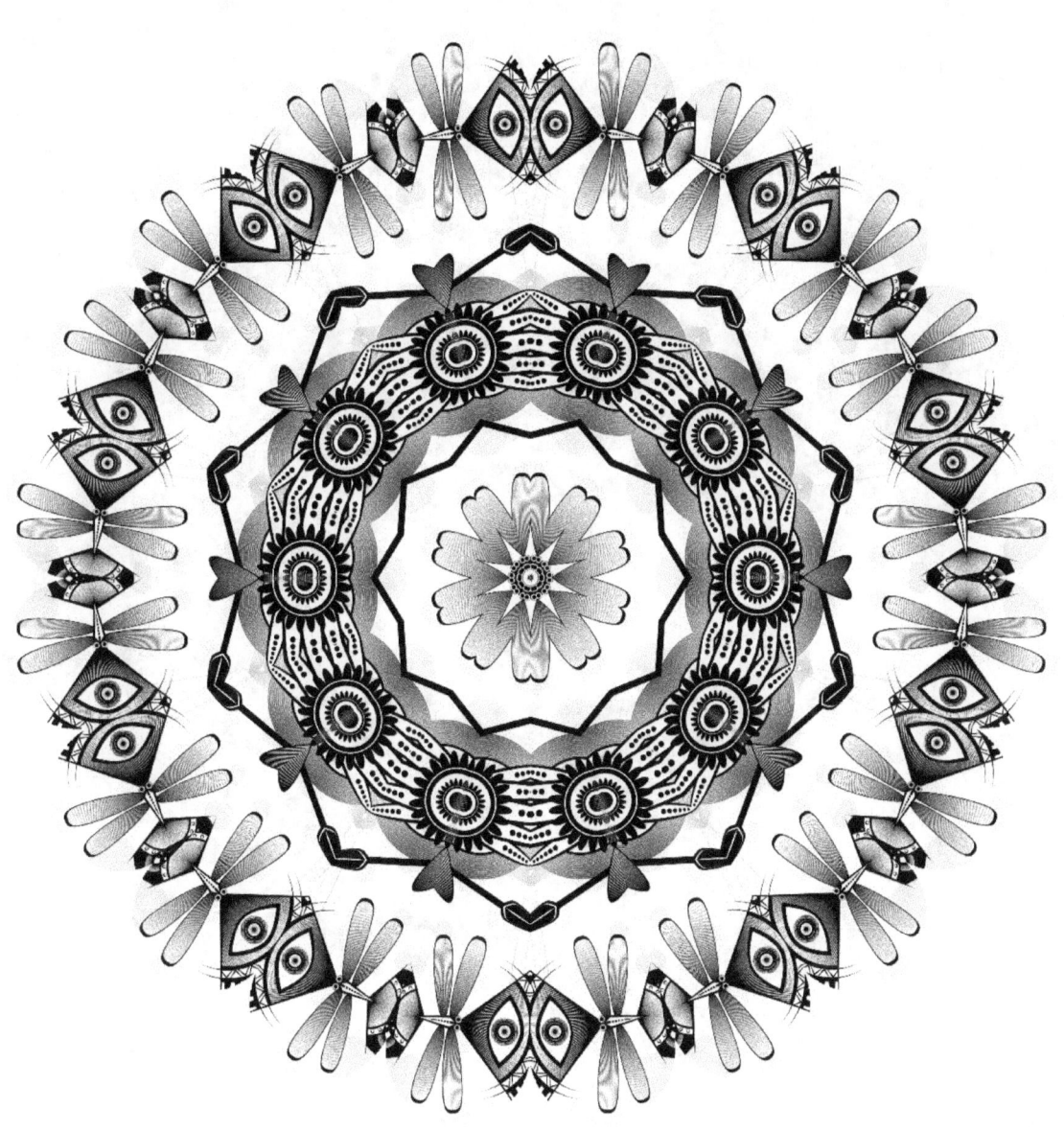

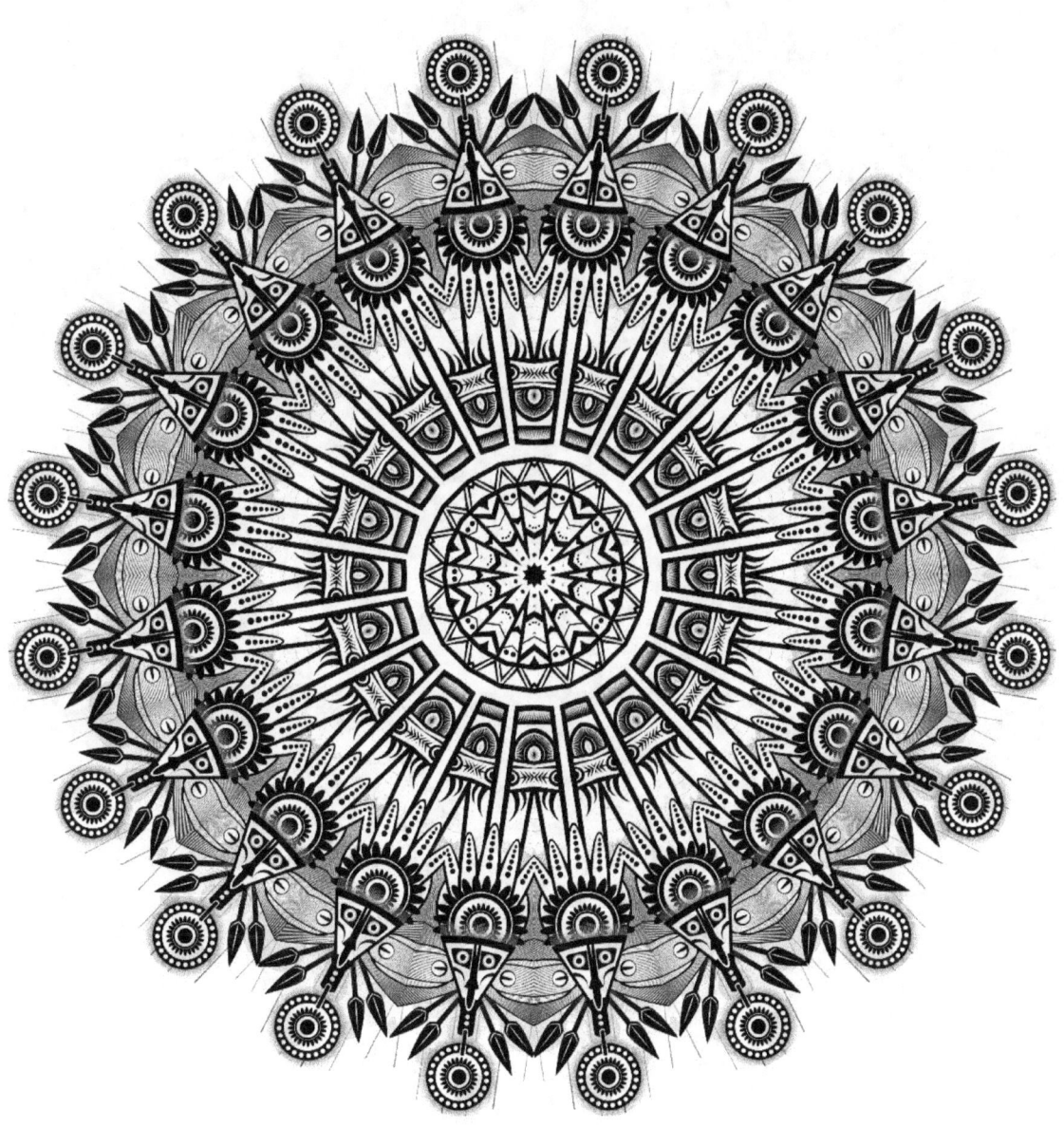

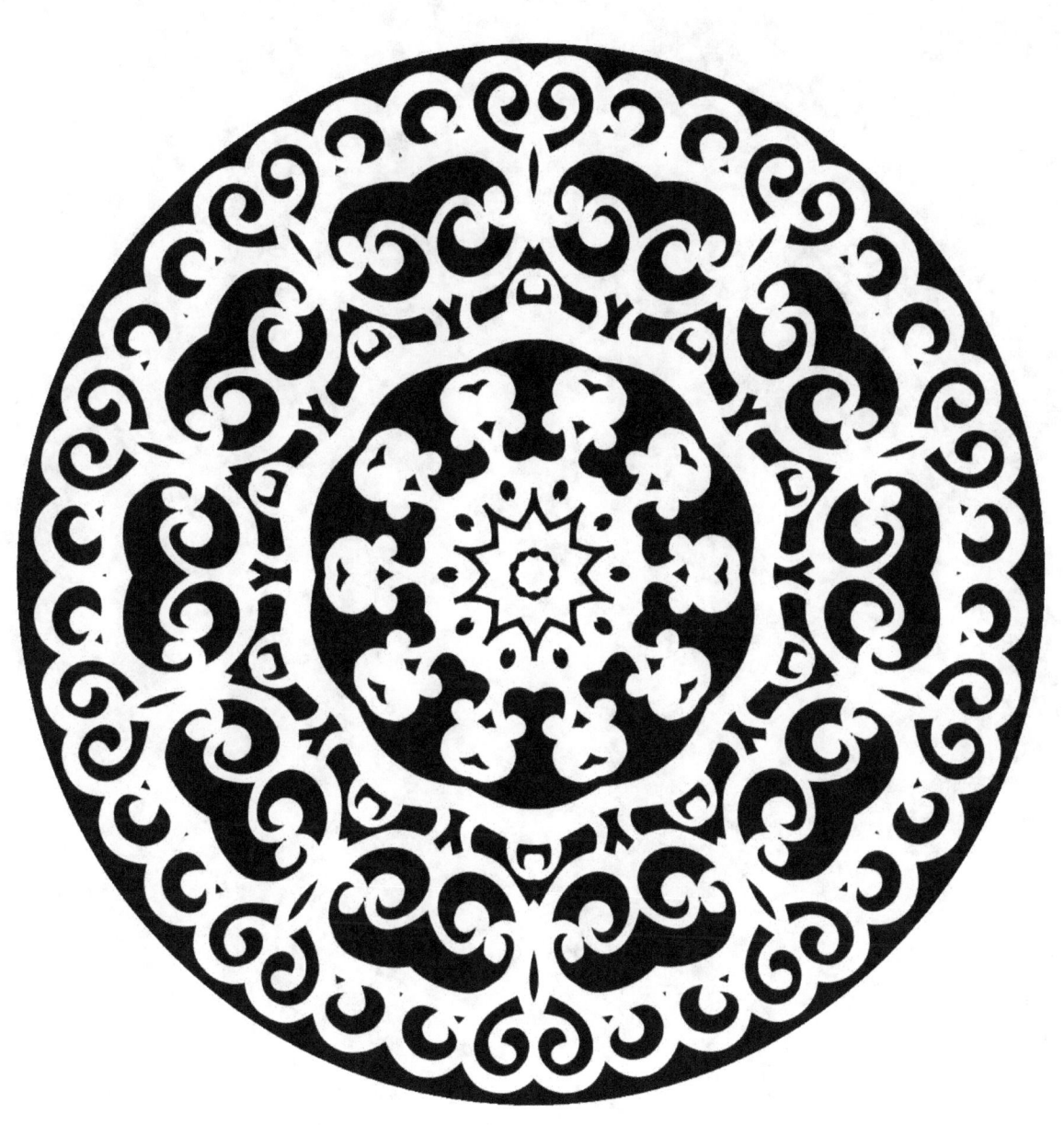

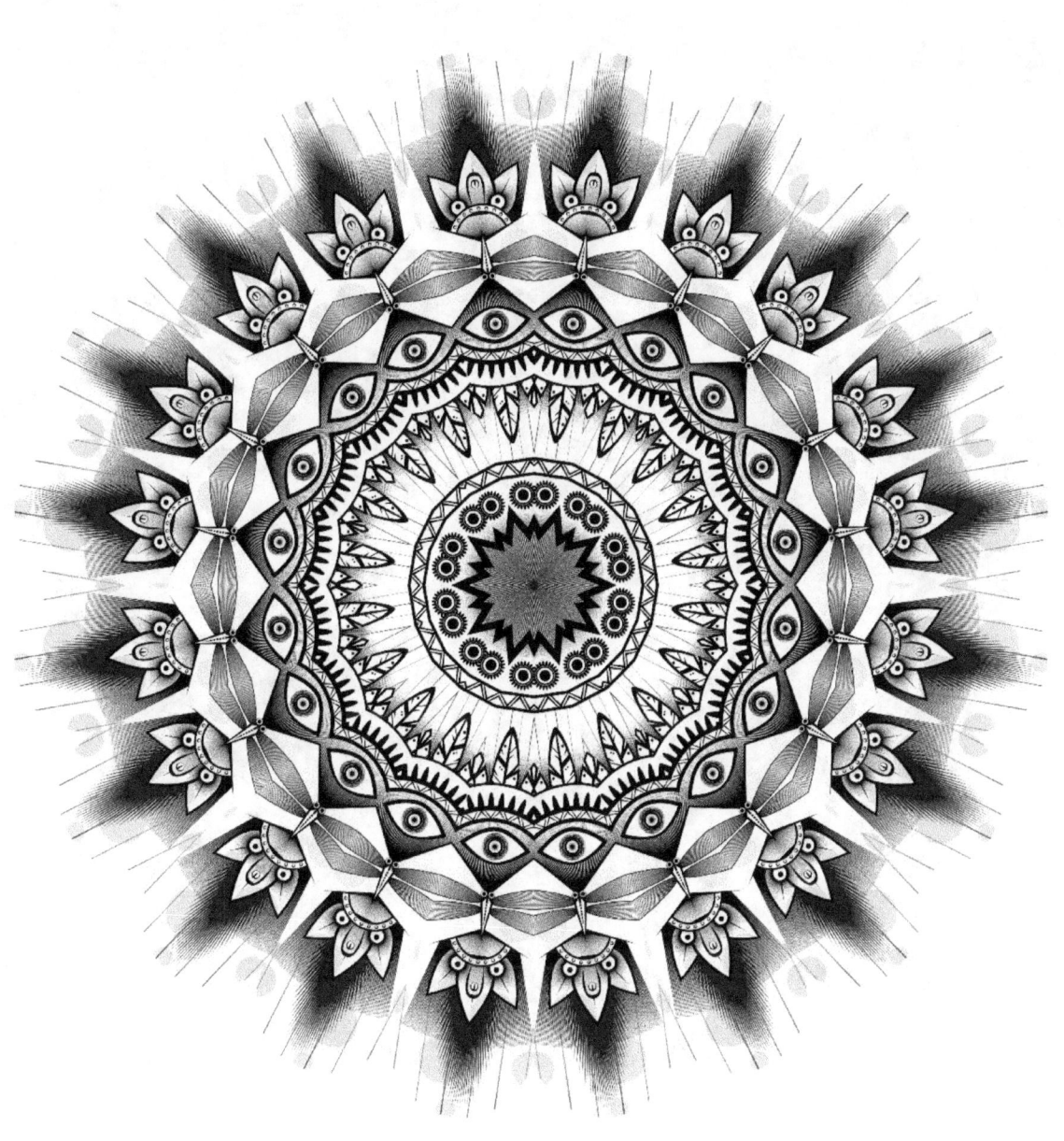

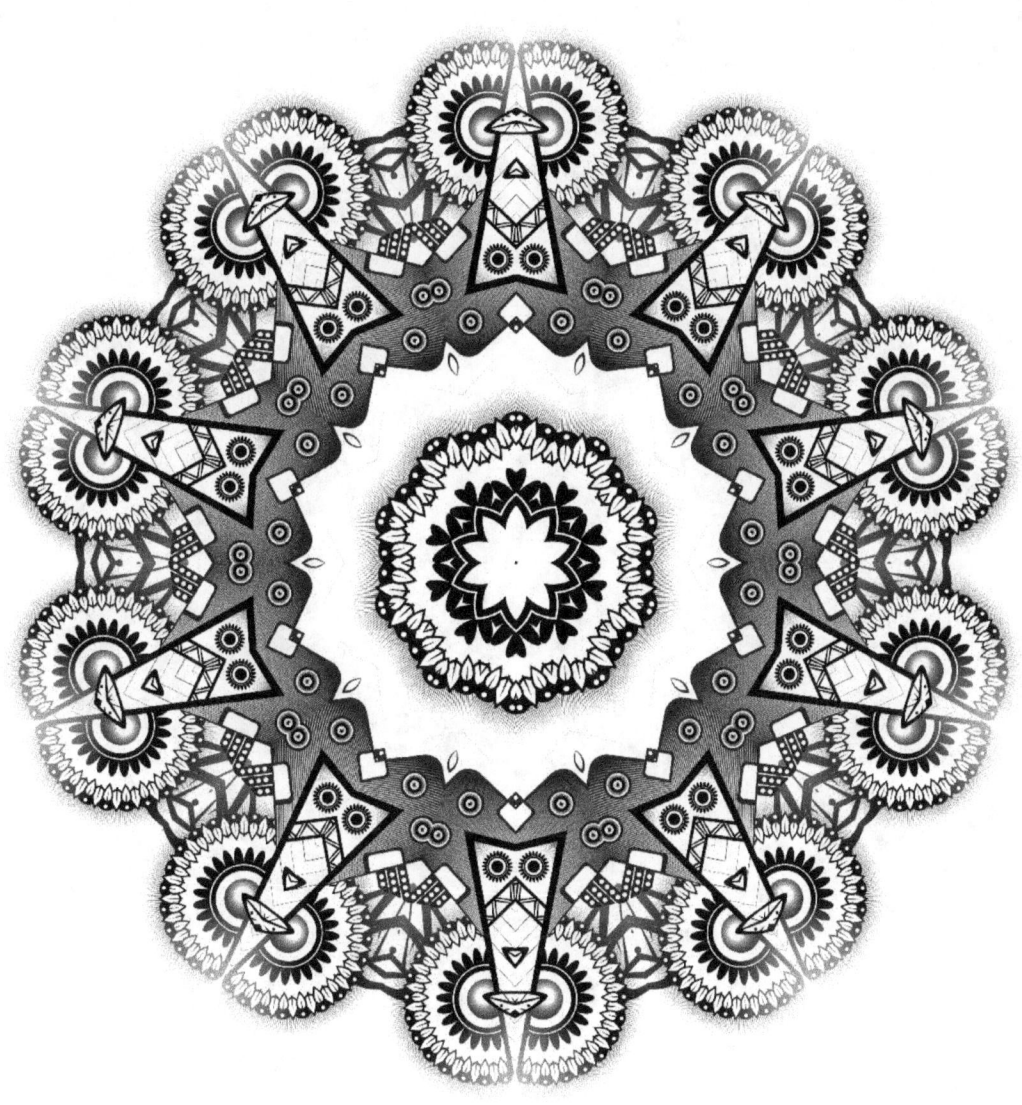

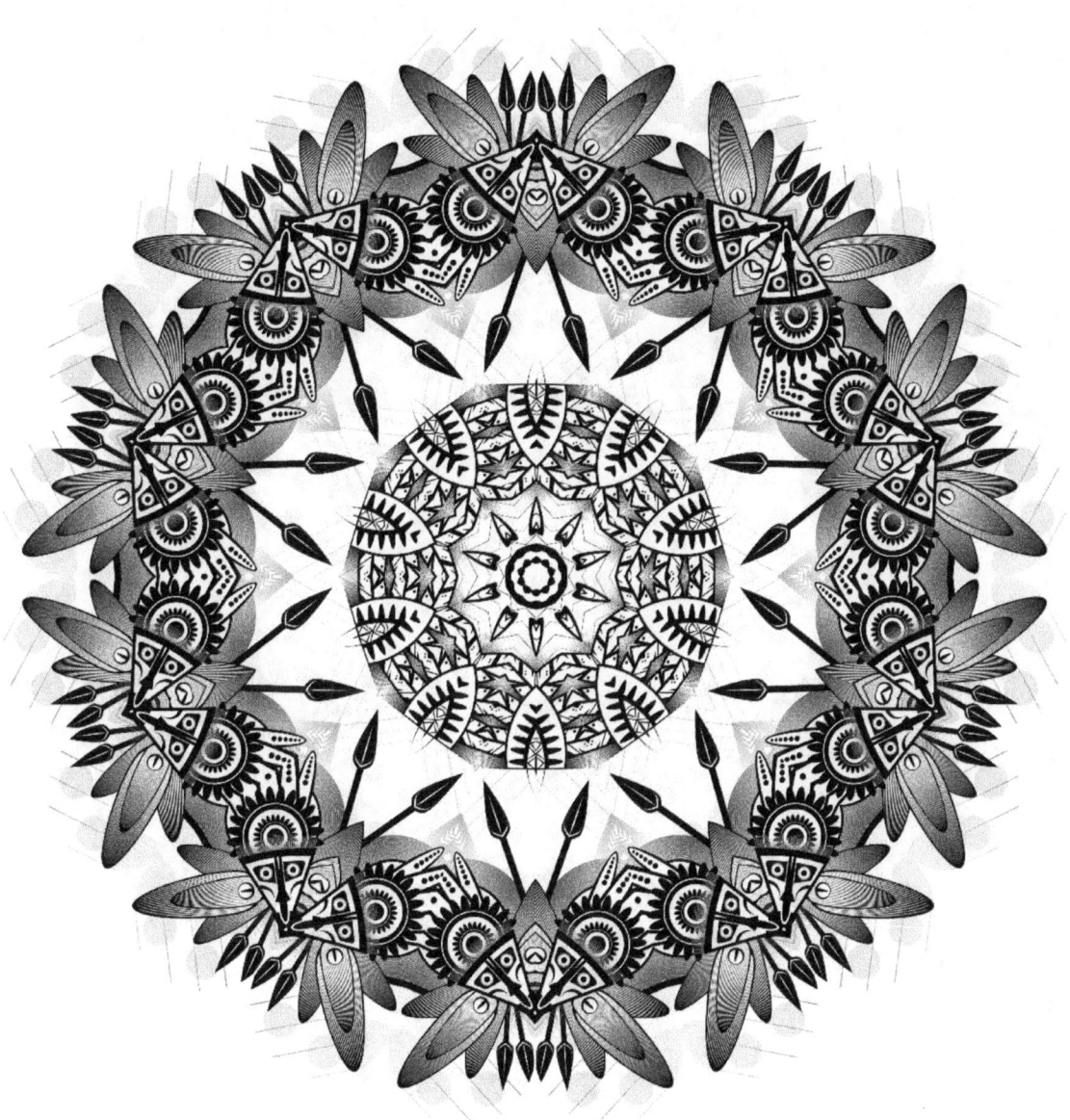

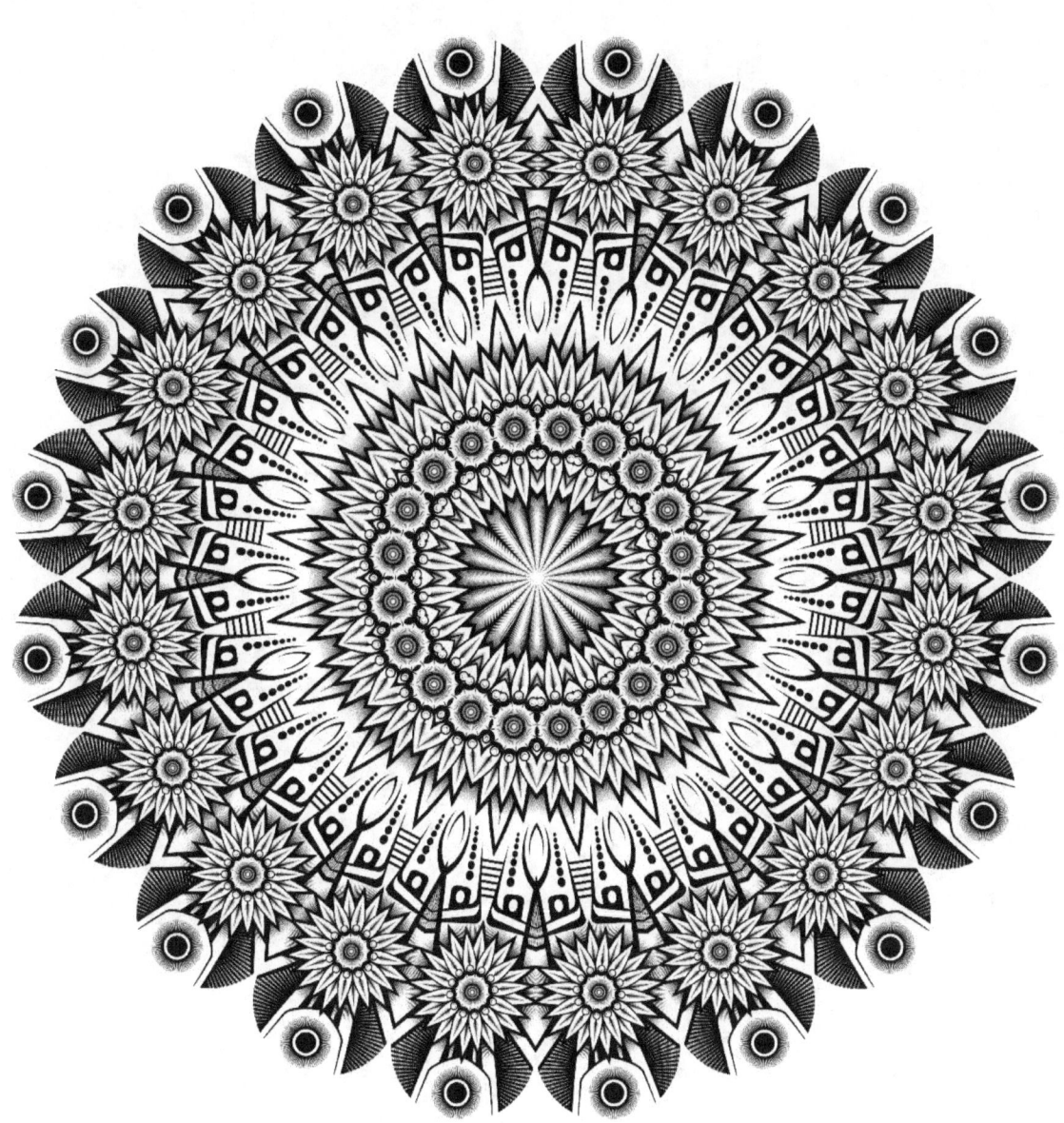

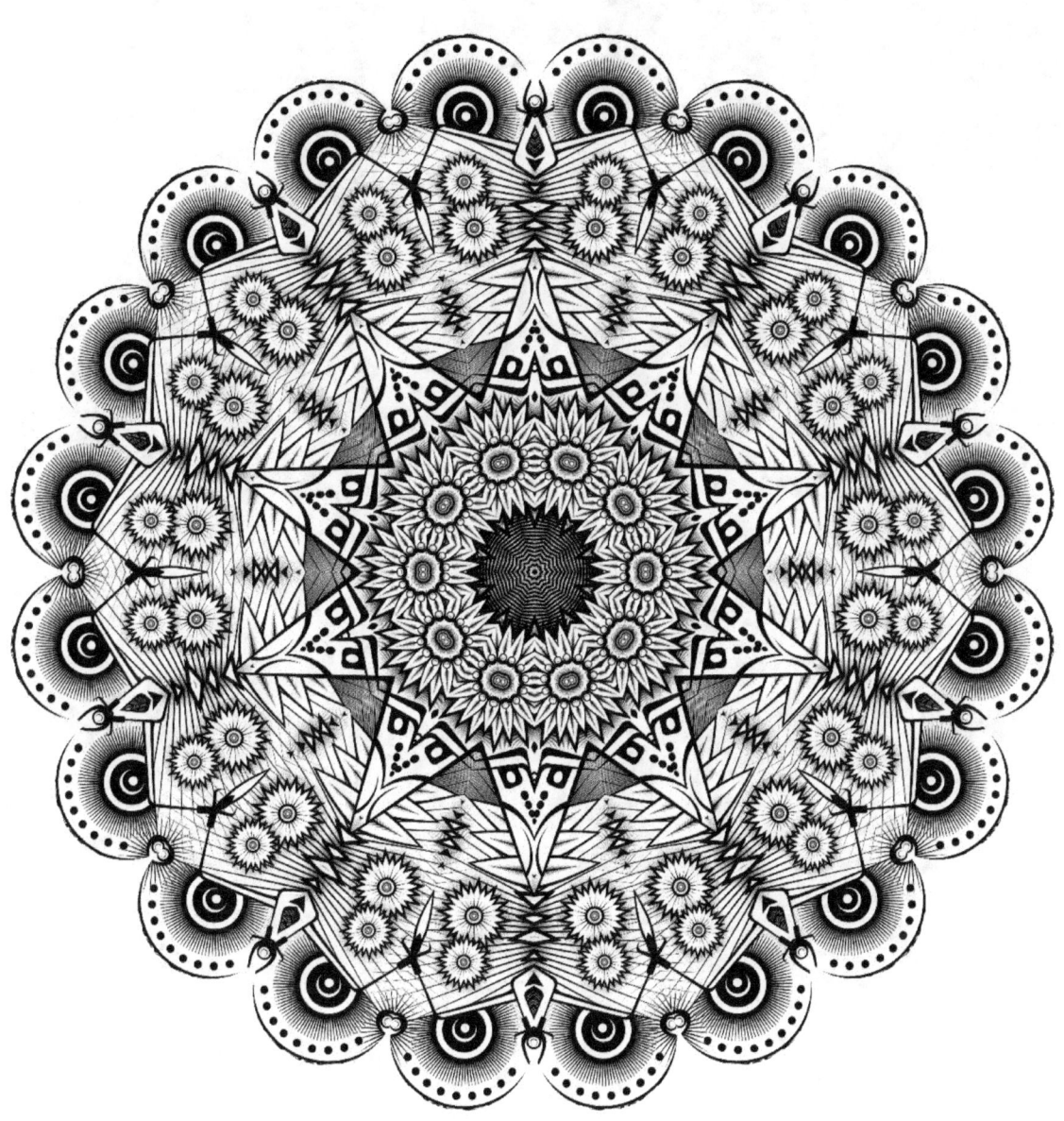

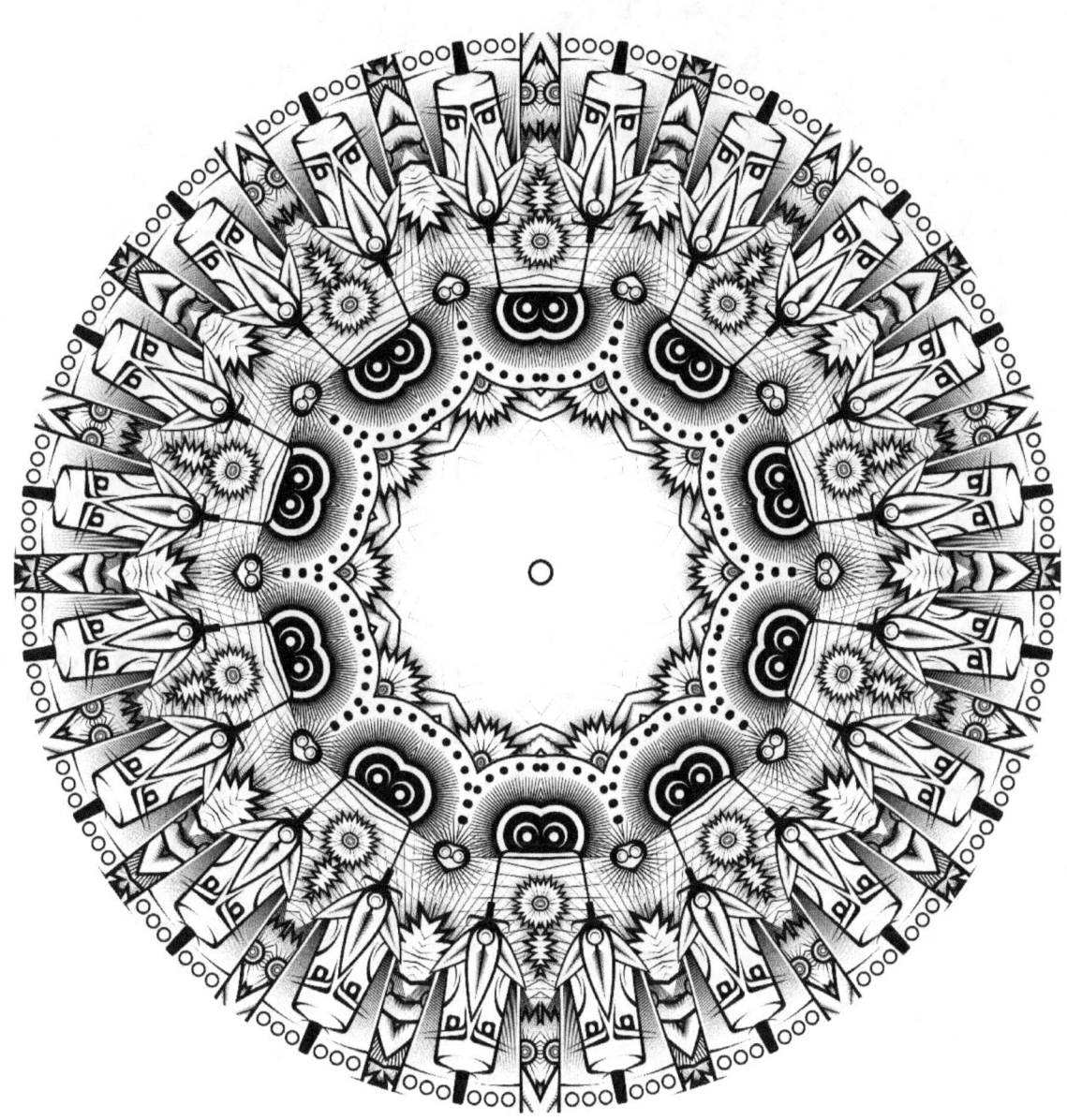

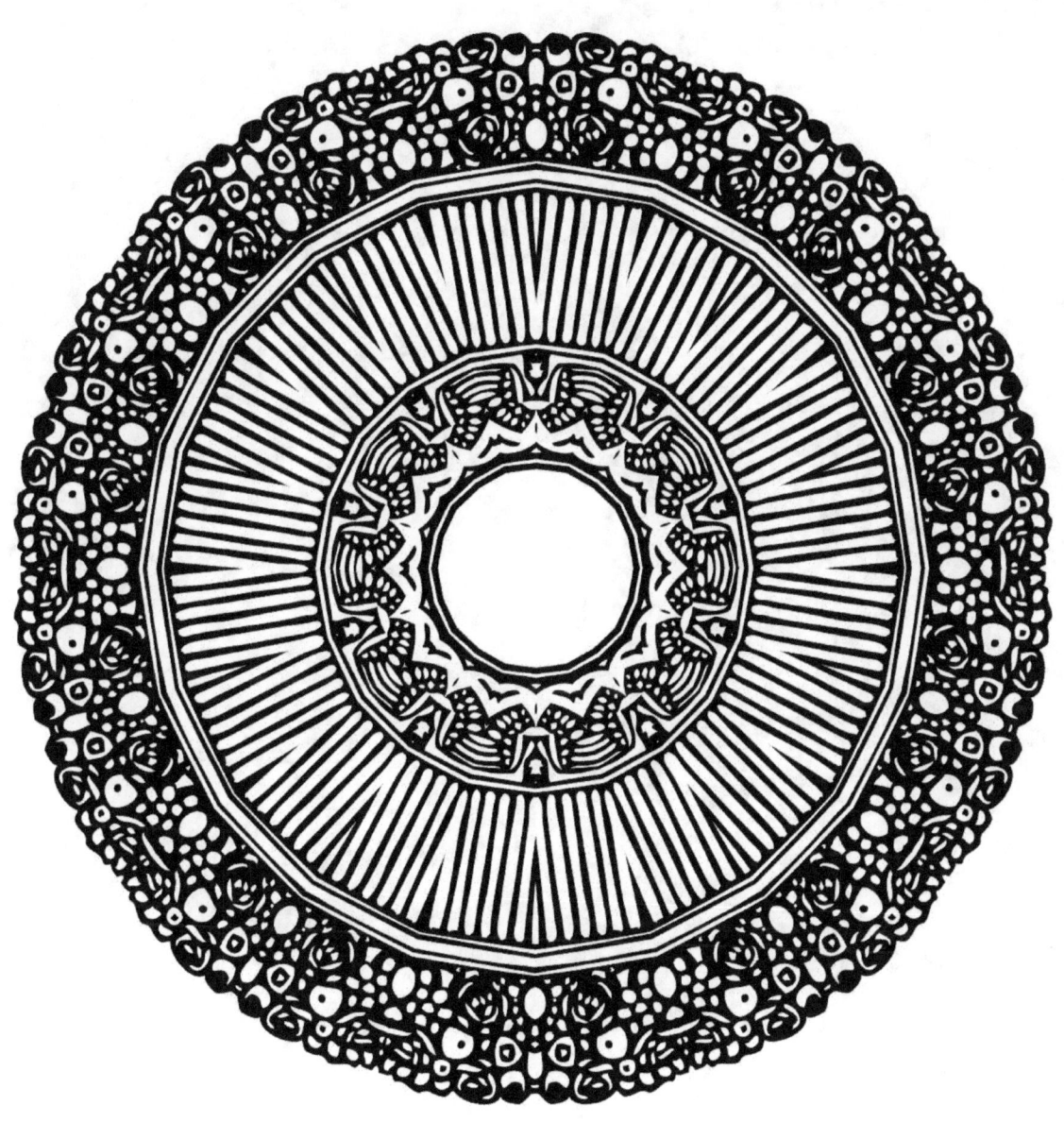

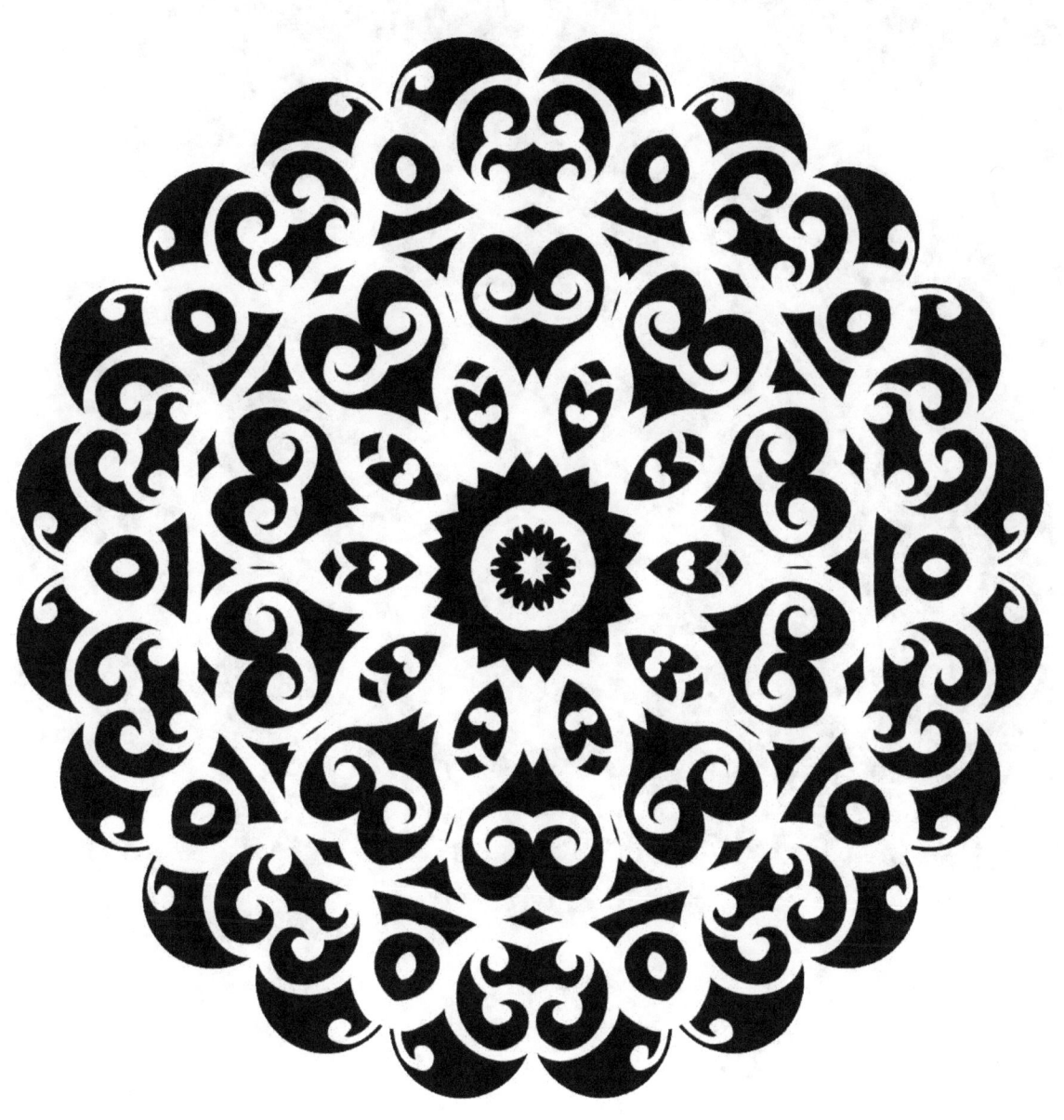

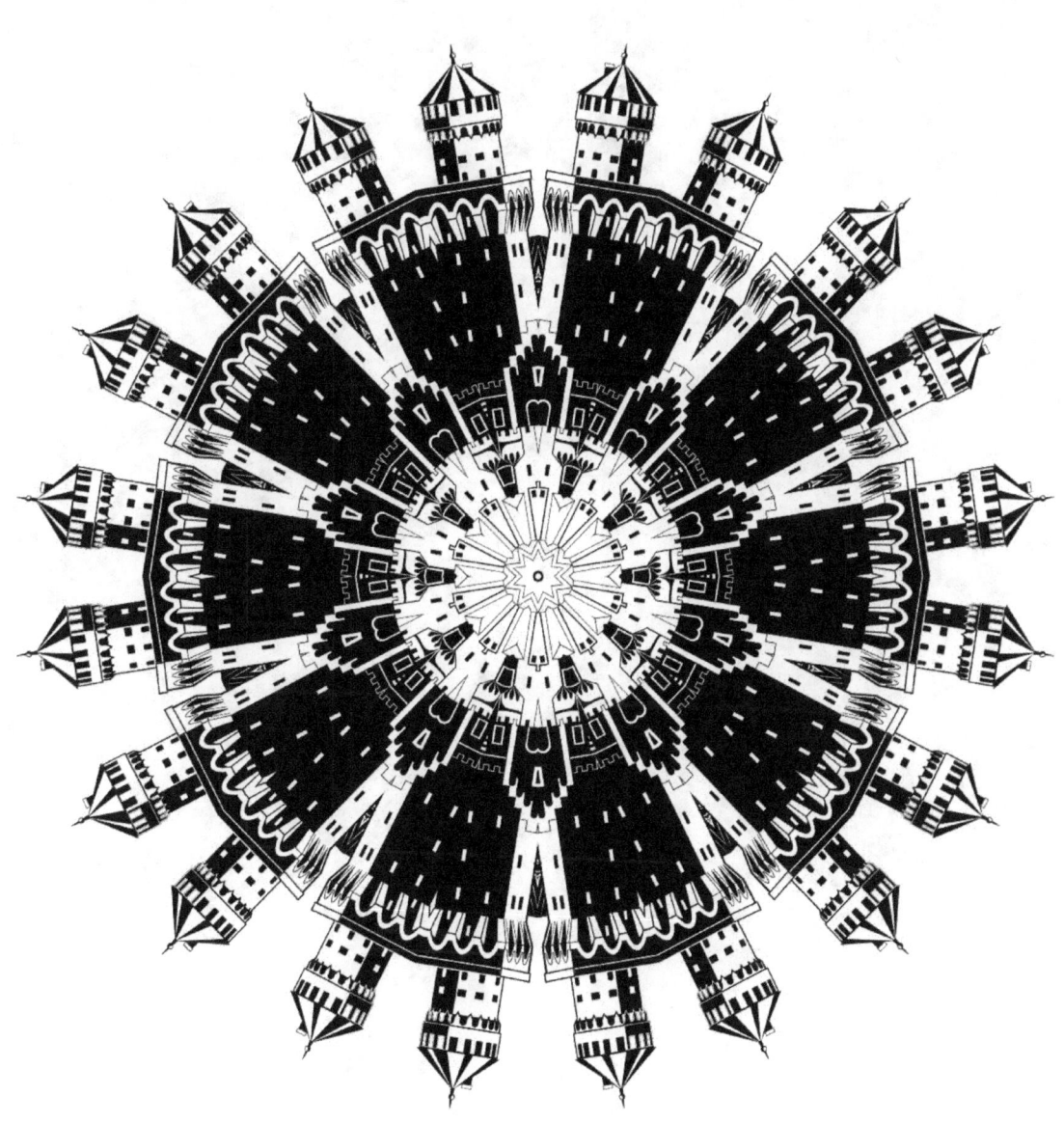

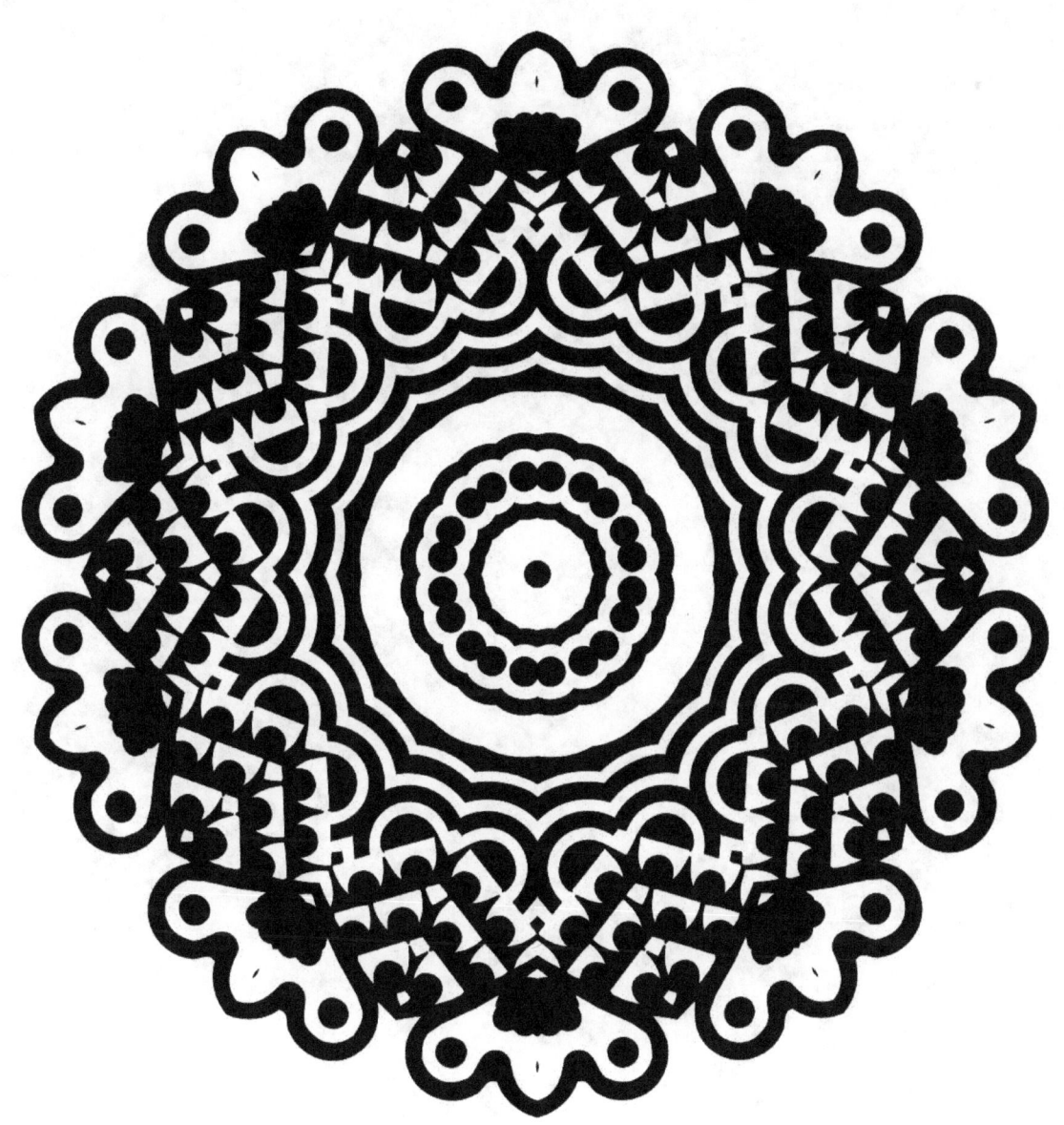

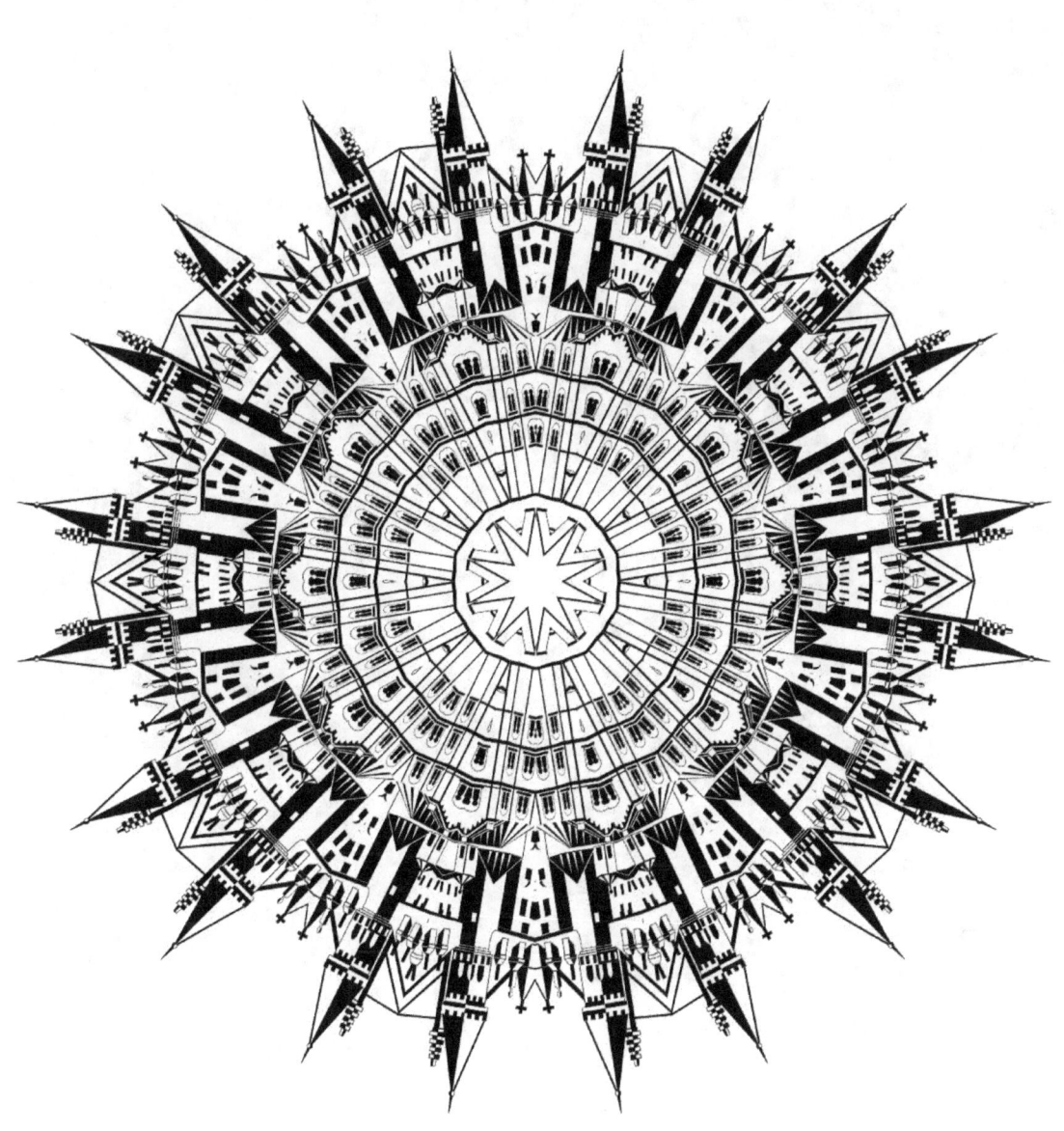

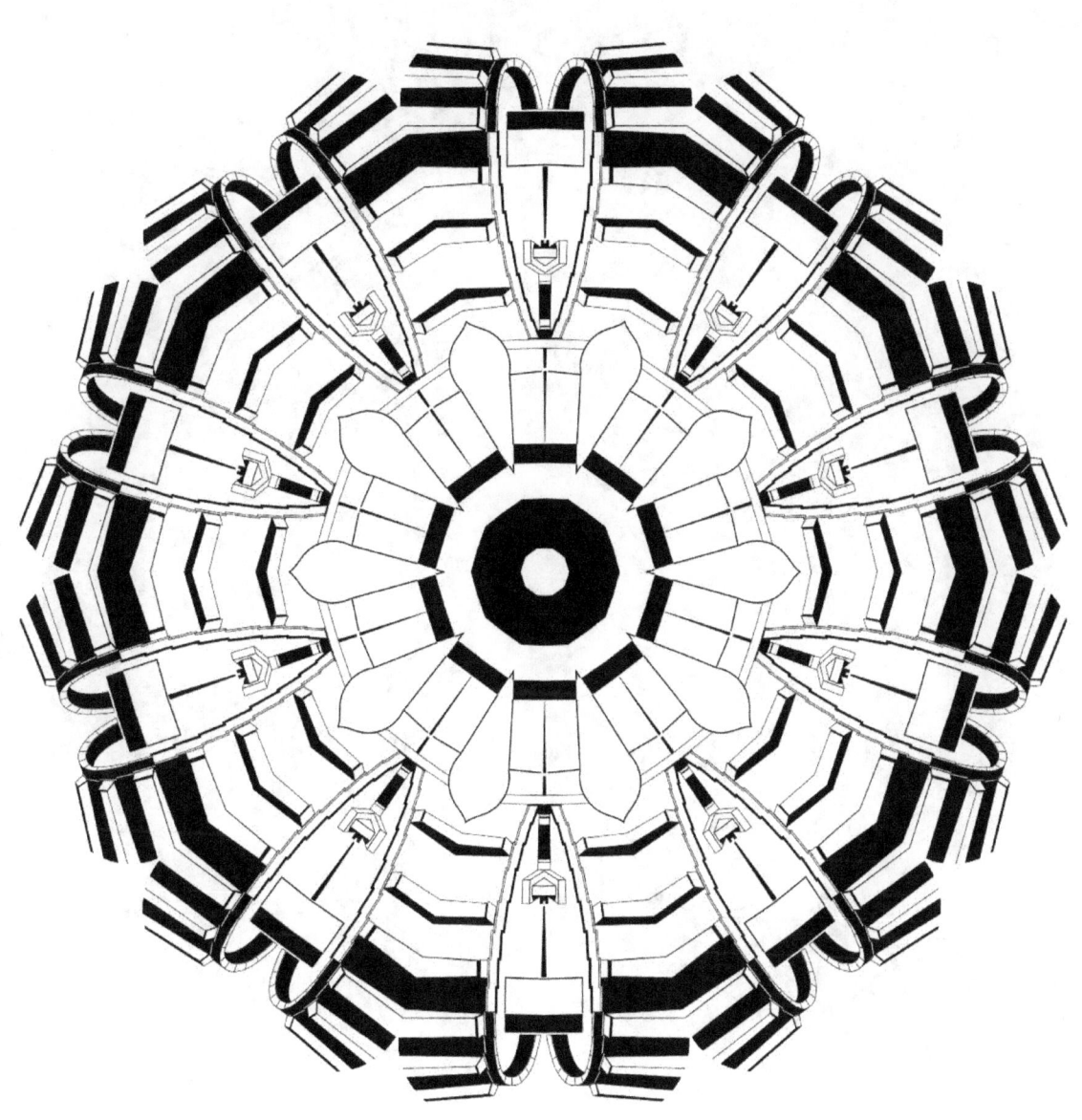

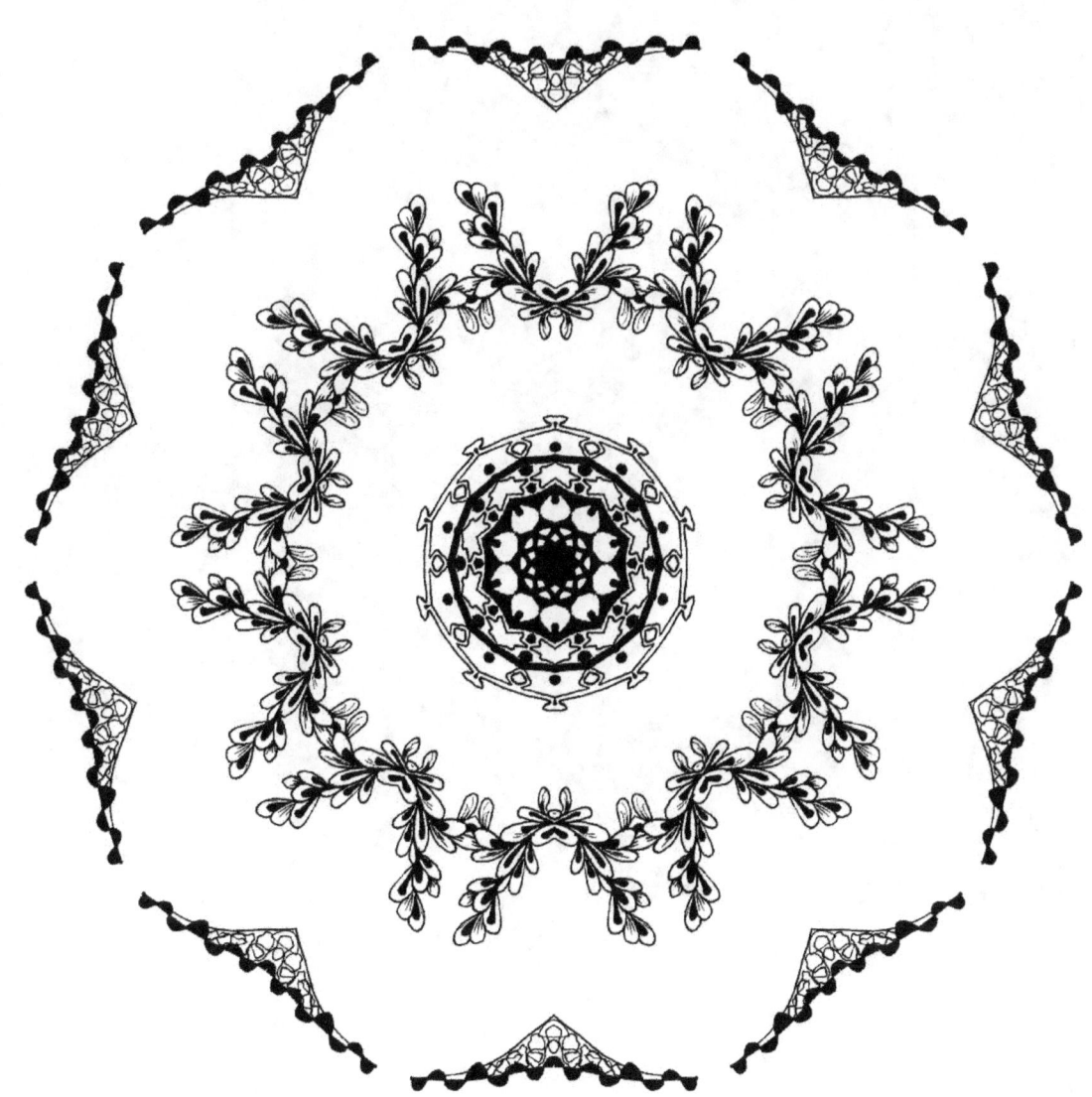

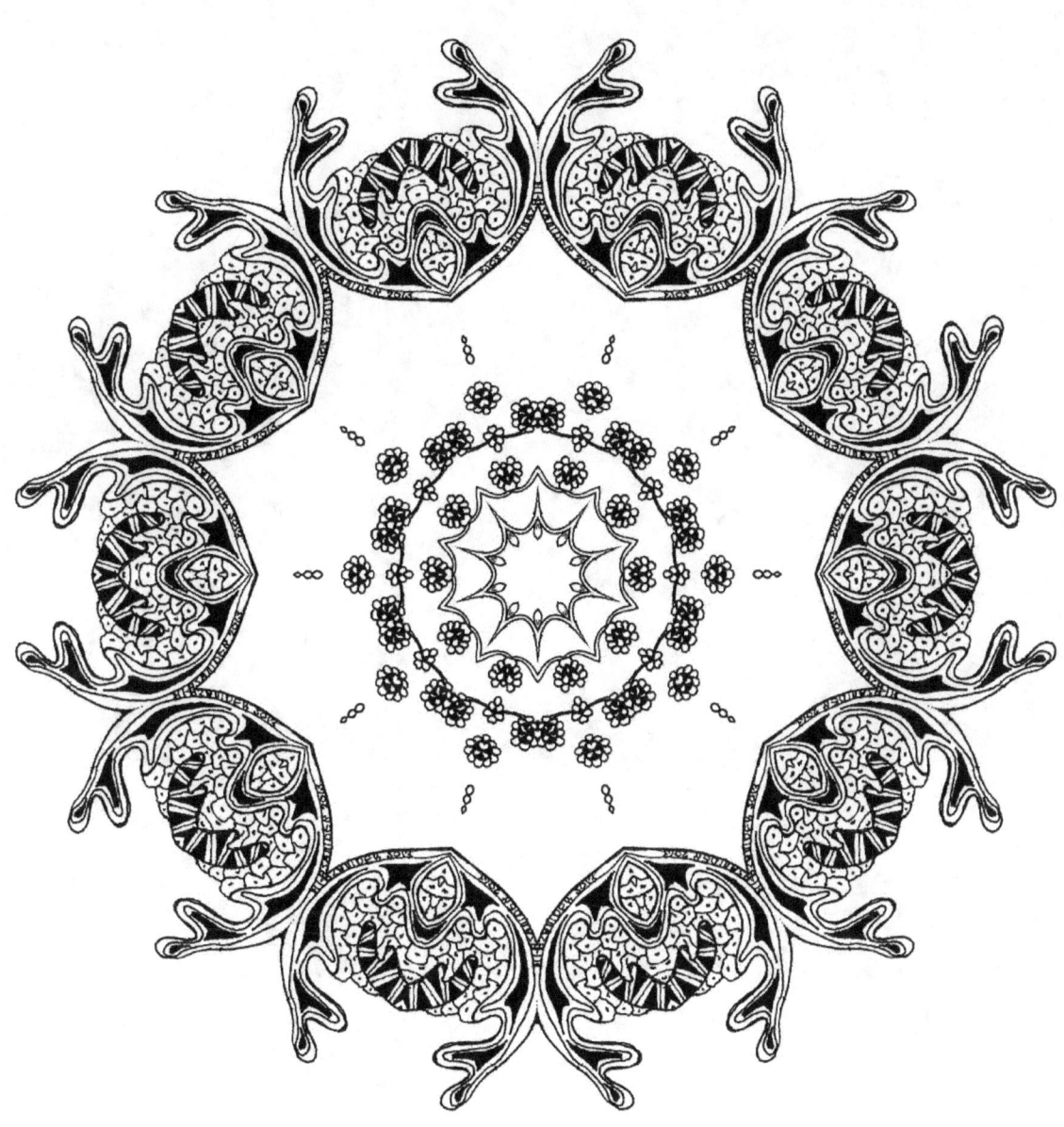

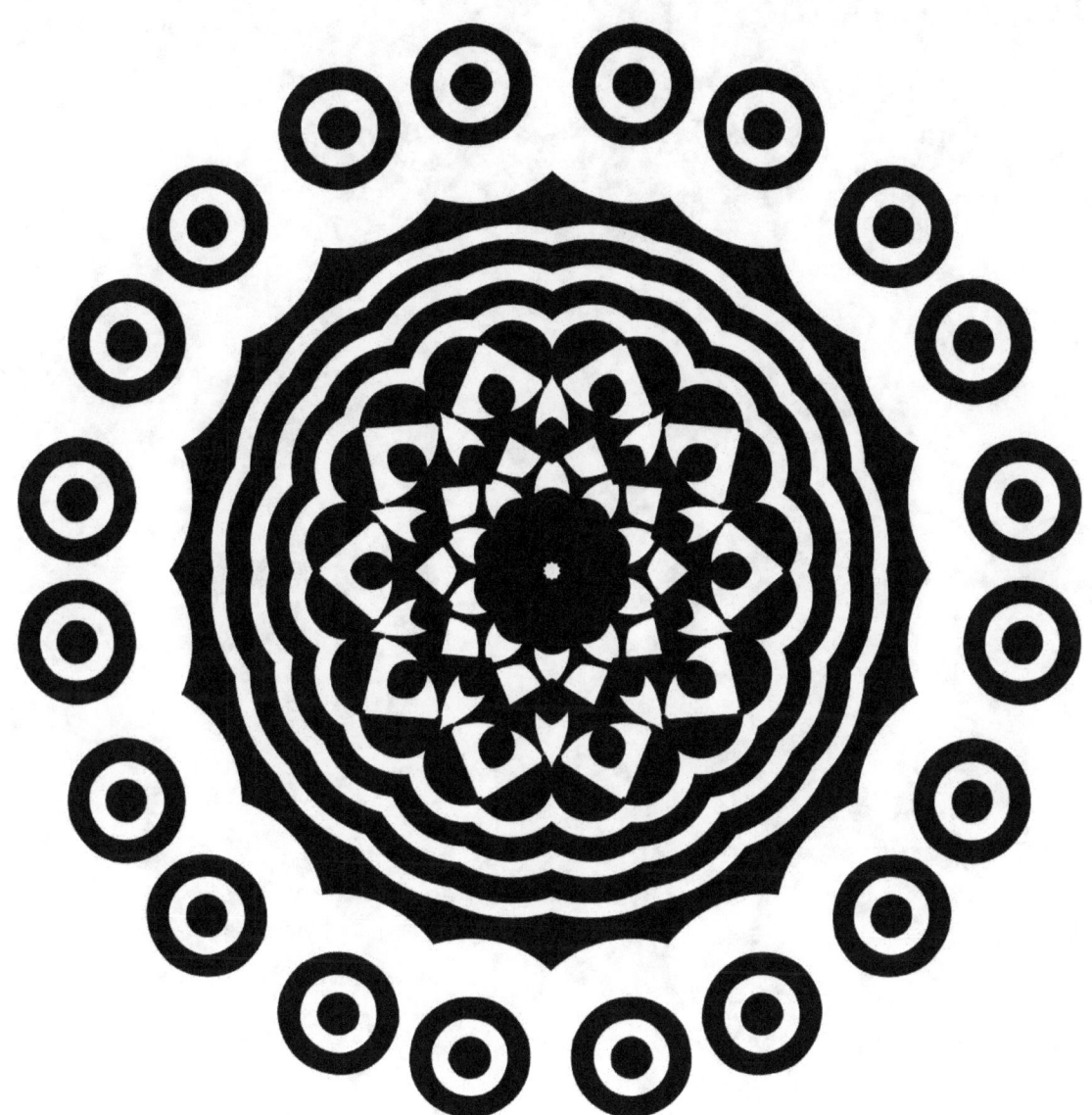

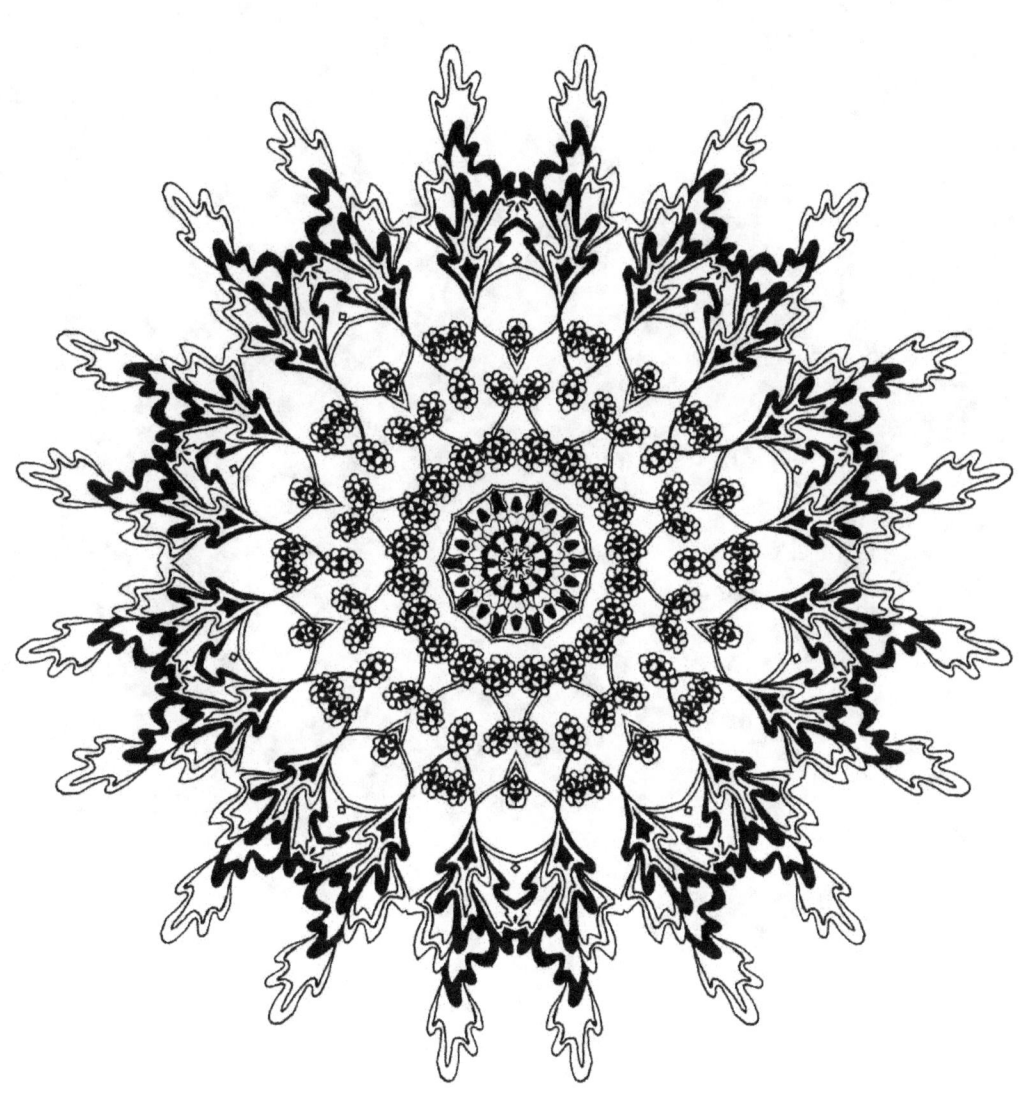

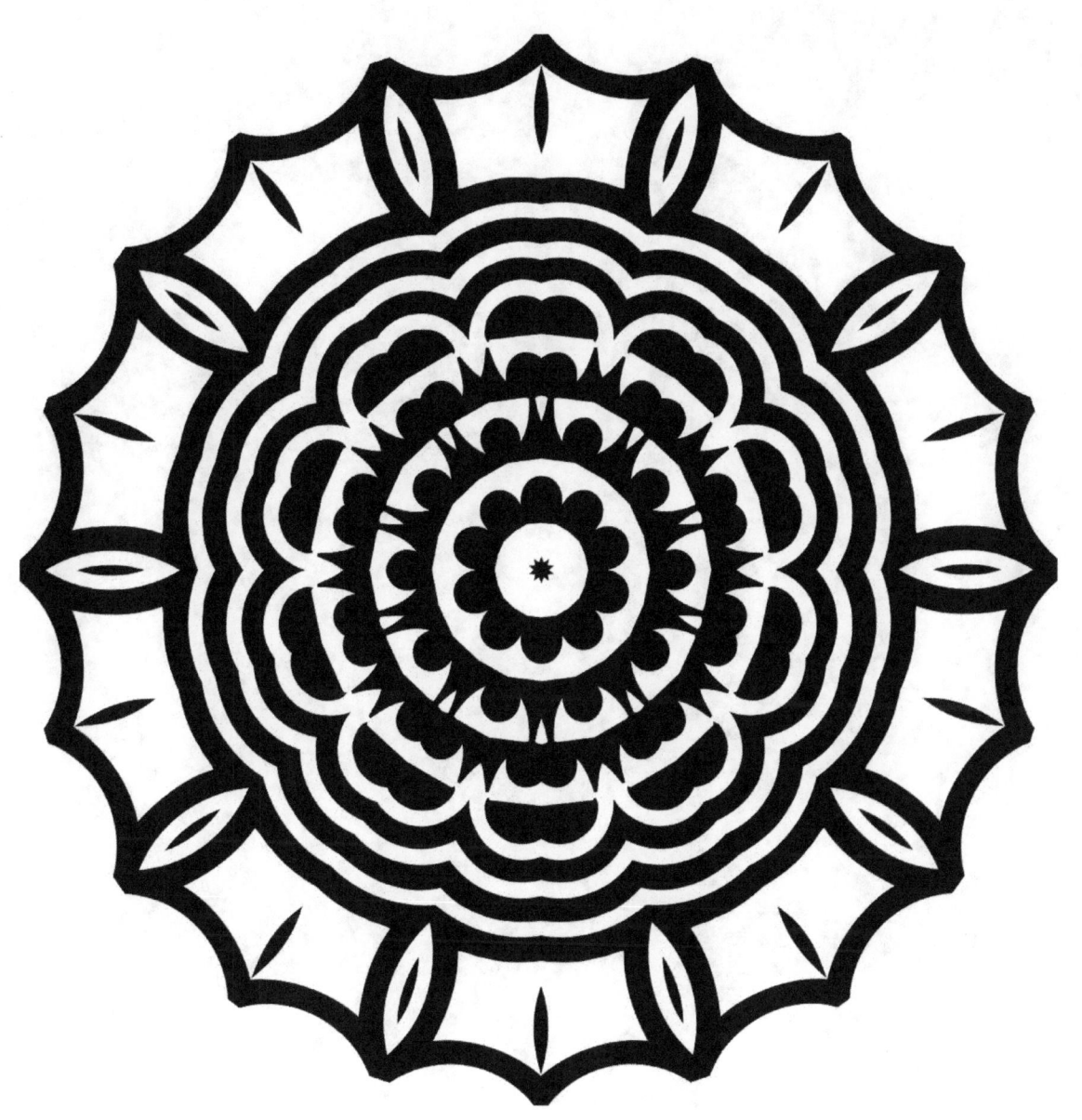

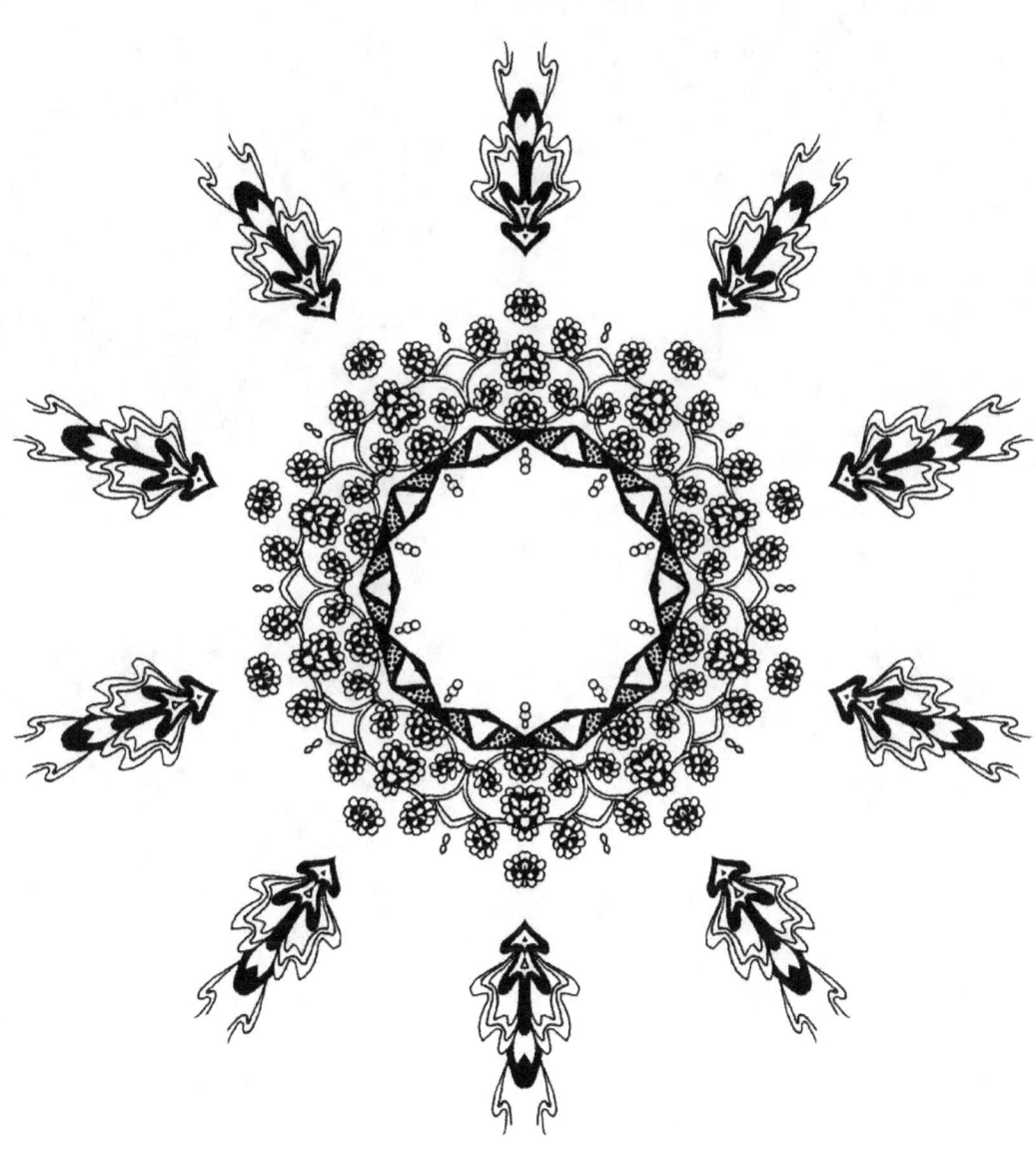

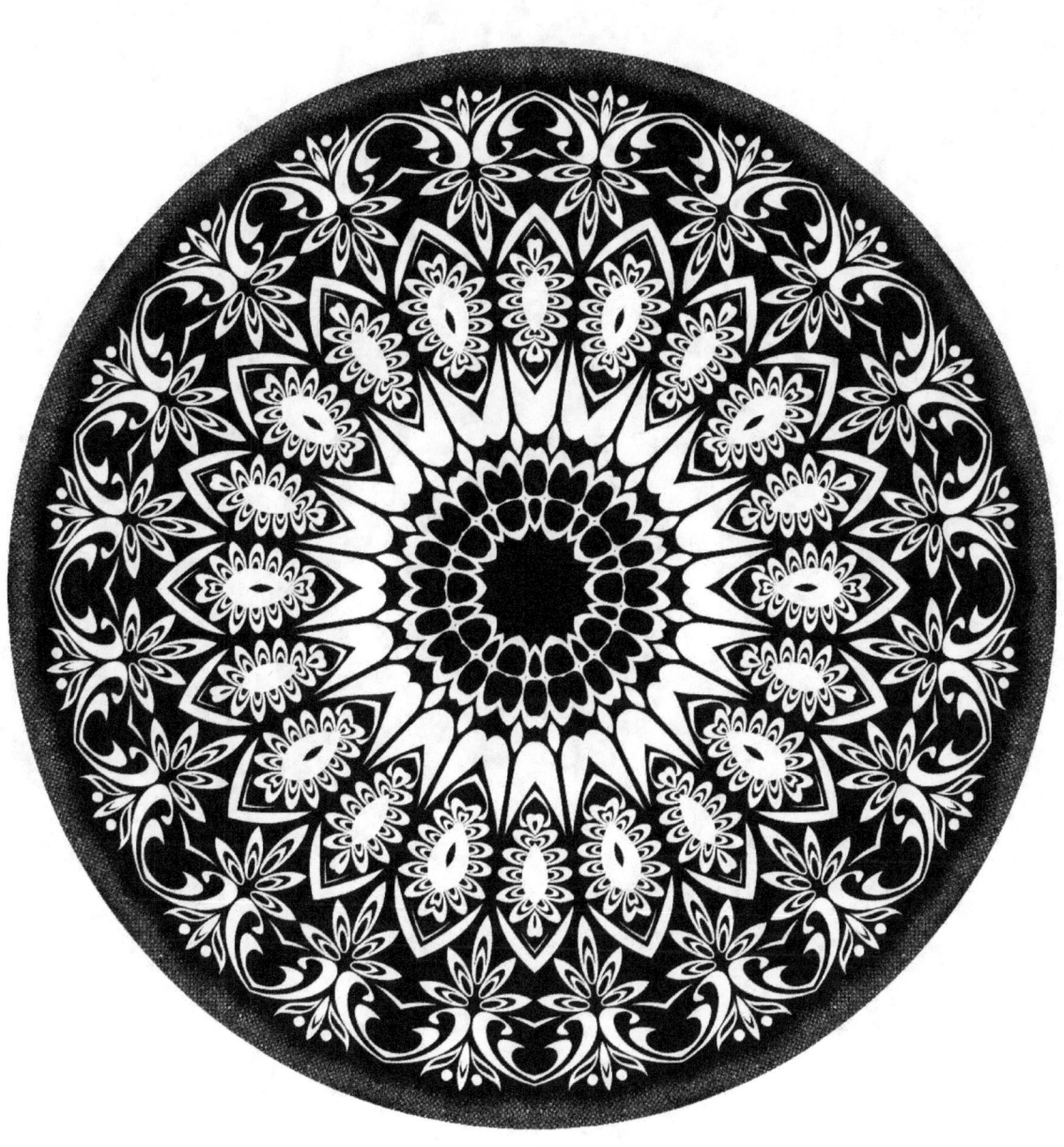

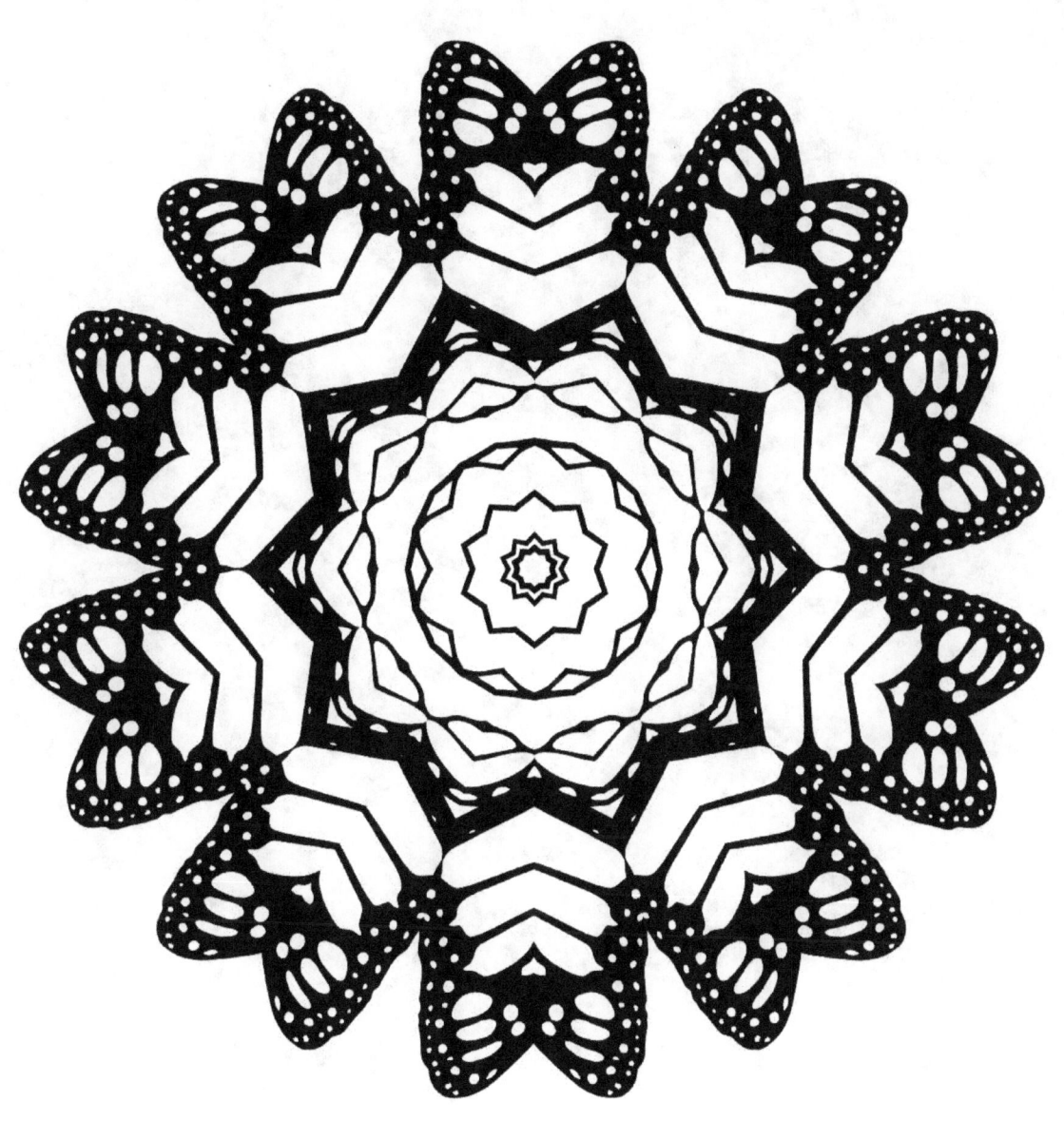

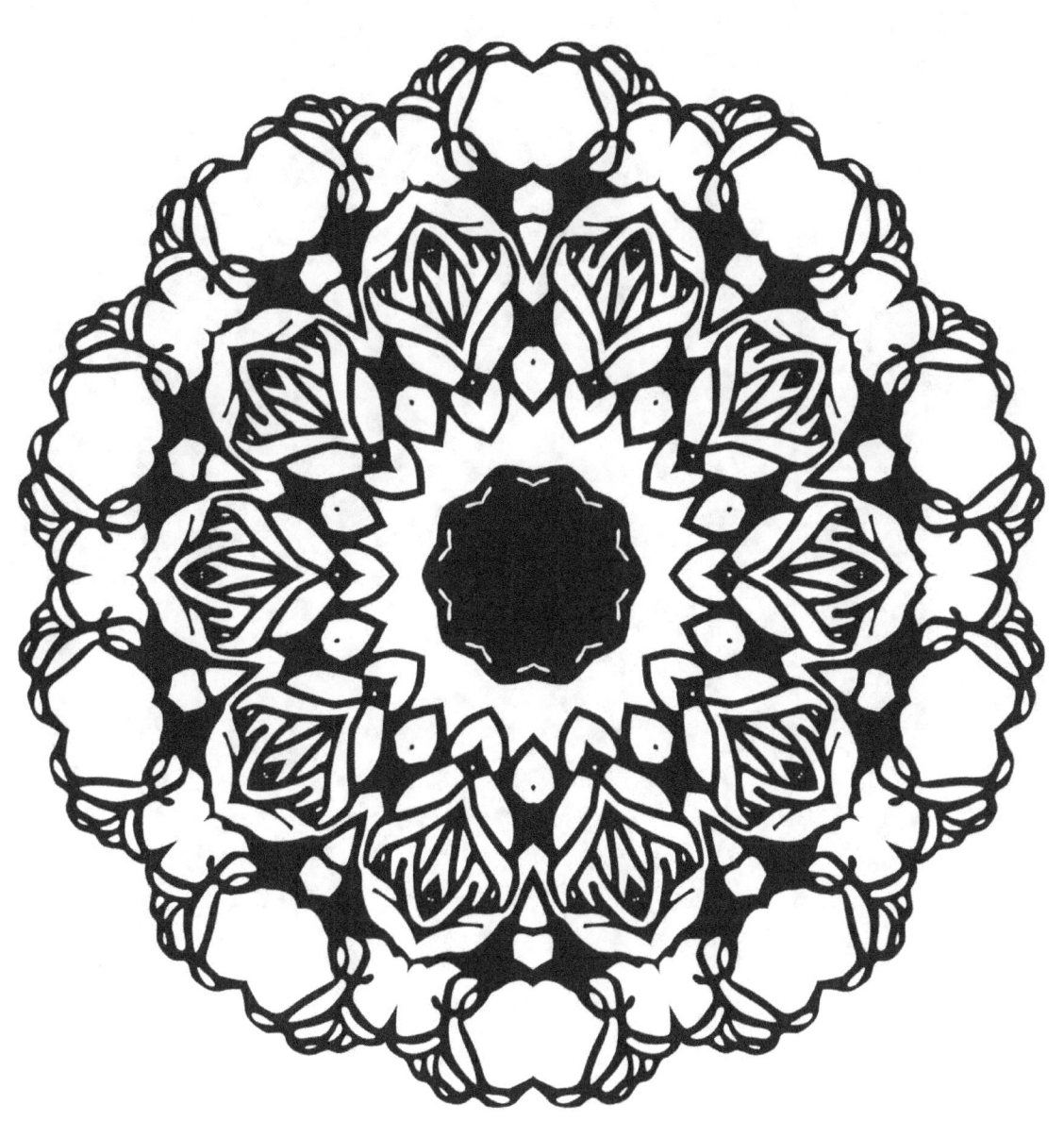

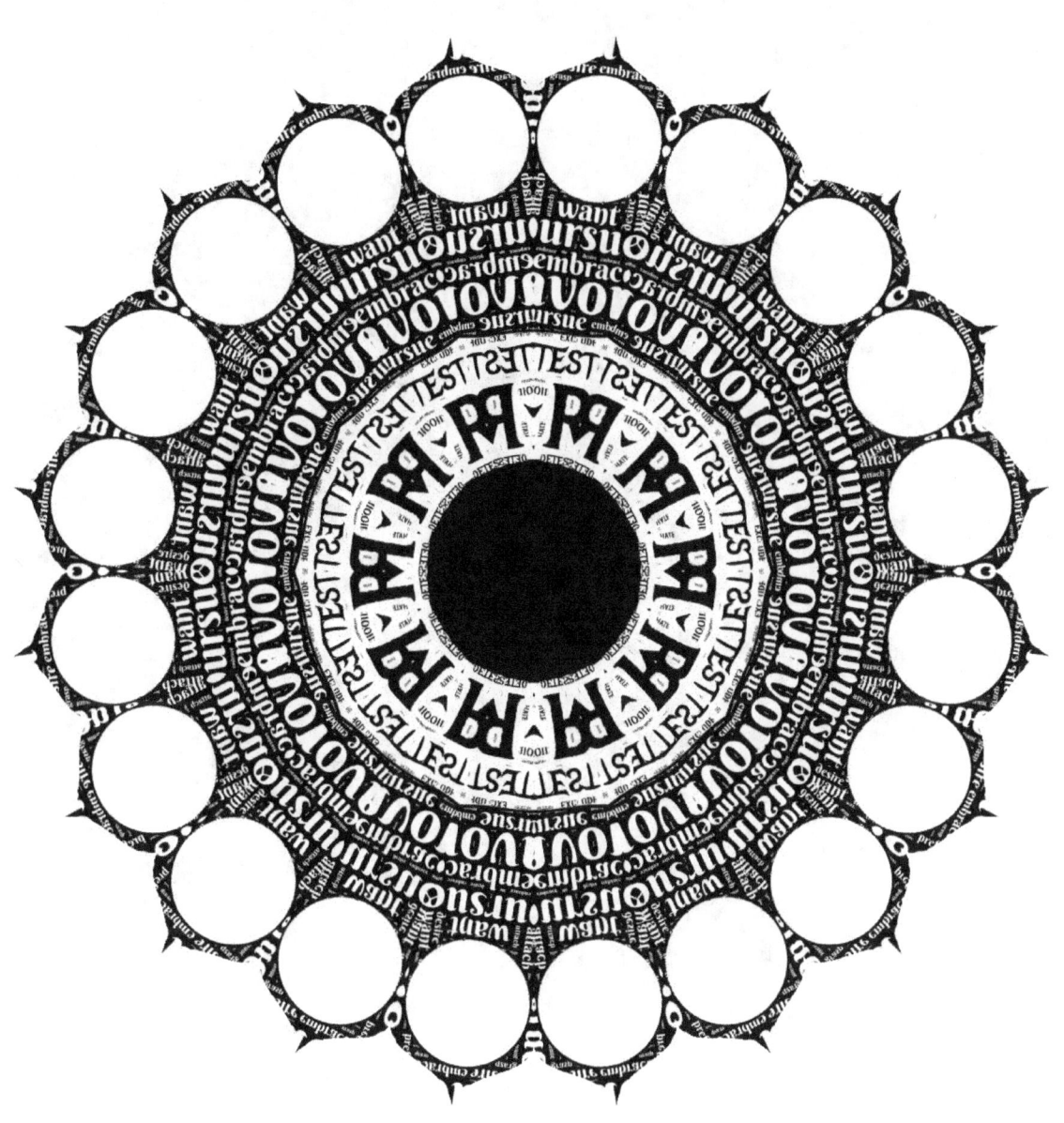